The Beginner's Guide to

COIN
COLLECTING

JAMES MACKAY

GALLERY BOOKS
An imprint of W.H. Smith Publishers Inc.
112 Madison Avenue
New York, New York 10016

A QUINTET BOOK

Produced for
GALLERY BOOKS
an imprint of W. H. Smith Publishers, Inc.
112 Madison Avenue
New York, New York 10016

ISBN 0–8317–0749–6

This book was designed and produced by
Quintet Publishing Limited
6 Blundell Street
London N7 9BH

Creative Director: Terry Jeavons
Designer: Chris Dymond
Artwork: Danny McBride
Project Editor: Damian Thompson,
Henrietta Wilkinson
Editor: Lesley M. Young
Photographer: Trevor Wood

Typeset in Great Britain by
Central Southern Typesetters, Eastbourne
Manufactured in Hong Kong by
Regent Publishing Services Limited
Printed in Hong Kong by
Leefung-Asco Printers Limited

CONTENTS

Collecting Coins

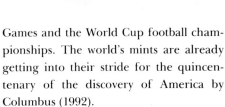

*C*oin collecting is a satisfying hobby that can be tailored to suit any-one's purse. In fact, anyone's purse may, at any given time, contain the nucleus of a collection! You can restrict your interests to current coins of your own country, collecting different dates and looking out for die variants in each denom-ination; or you can collect the coins of countries visited on business or vacation. The drawbacks of these approaches are that you will end up with a diverse collection and many of your specimens may not be in the best condition. Nowadays many coun-tries provide a new issue service to collectors through their mints and numismatic bureaux. When I began to collect coins seriously, I had to obtain international money orders and there were all kinds of restrictions on the import of coins, espe-cially gold coins. Today there are few re-strictions and the purchase can even be made merely by giving your credit card number on the order form.

You may decide to collect coins in a cer-tain metal, such as silver or bronze, or con-centrate on coins of a specific size. There are collectors who restrict their interest to minor coins (nickels and dimes, sixpences or shillings) and others who stick to dollars and crowns. Nowadays coins are infinitely more pictorial in design than ever and this has encouraged collecting along thematic lines. Fauna and flora, historic events and personalities, ships, locomotives, auto-mobiles and even space travel have been featured on modern coins. You can collect the coins of 1980–90 from many countries celebrating the 80th, 85th and 90th birth-days of the Queen Mother, or other royal events such as coronations, weddings and jubilees; or you may prefer coins celebrating sporting events, such as the Olympic Games and the World Cup football cham-pionships. The world's mints are already getting into their stride for the quincen-tenary of the discovery of America by Columbus (1992).

Many collectors in Britain concentrate on the numismatics of their own town or county, hunting for examples of silver pennies from the medieval mints, the elu-sive (and now rather expensive) coins from the English Civil War temporary mints or even the obsidional currency struck at Car-lisle, Newark, Pontefract and Scarborough when these towns were besieged by the Roundheads. There are also many who collect the very prolific tokens of the seven-teenth to nineteenth centuries.

CONDITION

Condition is by far the most important fac-tor in determining the value of a coin. Beginners are often surprised to discover that an enormous differential exists between a coin in flawless mint condition and one similar in every respect but showing the marks of circulation. Take the British 1949 nickel-brass threepence, for example. In average circulated condition it would be worth about £1.50 today. In Very Fine (VF) condition it rates twice as much, but in Ex-tremely Fine (EF) condition it rates £35, and for a superb, uncirculated example with its original lustre intact, you would expect to pay anything from £100 to £135. Condition is therefore a vital factor and it is important for the collector to understand what it means.

Above: Coins depicting buildings from Iceland (Parliament, Reykjavik), Thailand (Royal Palace, Bangkok), Macau (ruins of St Paul's Cathedral), Malaysia (Parliament, Kuala Lumpur) and Indonesia (Menangkabu traditional dwelling-house).

Below: Birds on coins: Singapore (sea eagle), New Zealand (kiwi), Greece (owl), Cambodia (garuda), Vatican (peace dove), Gibraltar (Barbary partridge), Cook Islands (fairy tern or fairylake swallow) and Isle of Man (peregrine falcon).

Above: Two late
seventeenth-century
numismatists studying
their coins. Note the
elaborate baroque coin
cabinet, with its narrow
drawers, in the
background. (From an
engraving in *La Science
des Médailles*, by Louis
Joubert, Paris, 1693.)

Proofs – Expect the Best

Normally, the condition factor must be taken in conjunction with the degree of scarcity. Although Roman coins exist in EF condition, the collector in this field will generally have to lower his or her sights or give up collecting. For modern coins, however, the condition of a coin is paramount. Of course there are great rarities, such as the 1952 half crown, the only known example of which had obviously been in circulation for years before an eagle-eyed change-checker spotted it. But modern coins, especially those that are still current, should not be collected unless they are in perfect condition.

Because of the highly mechanized nature of coin production, it is virtually impossible to obtain a freshly minted circulating coin in absolutely perfect condition, but when it comes to proofs and coins packaged as uncirculated specimens, you have a right to expect the best. General circulating coins, even when fresh from the mint, will be found to have minute edge knocks and surface blemishes caused as they tumble from the press and are bagged up.

The Grading System

Apart from proofs, the various grades of condition that the collector will encounter in auction catalogues and dealers' lists are as follows:

Fleur de coin (usually abbreviated to FDC) is synonymous with the American expression **Brilliant Uncirculated** (BU or B. Unc.). The only modern coins likely to be found in this state are proofs.

Uncirculated (Unc.) is the highest grade normally applied to a coin struck by standard mint machinery. A bronze penny in this grade should possess the brilliant copper-red lustre that distinguishes a newly minted coin. With age, this tends to darken attractively as the coin acquires a patina. This is caused by atmospheric oxidation and is, to put it crudely, a protective rust. It must be stressed that on no account should any attempt be made to remove the patina of a coin by polishing or abrasion. Such action, however well intentioned, is nothing short of vandalism and would effectively destroy the numismatic value of a coin. In uncirculated coins, even the most delicate hair-lines should be sharply defined.

Extremely Fine (EF) denotes a coin that is in a state of almost pristine perfection, but has been handled to some degree. It should have every detail of the engraving clearly delineated, but will probably have lost some of its original lustre.

Very Fine (VF) coins will have slight traces of wear on their highest surfaces. Points to watch for are the fine lines in the hair of the portrait or signs of wear on the truncation of the bust, the highest point of the obverse. Coins in VF condition are collectable only if no better specimens are easily obtainable. Collectors are sometimes tempted to buy coins in this, or lower, condition in order to fill gaps, but as VF coins will never have the resale potential of the higher grades, such purchases are often false economy.

COIN DEALERS
AND AUCTIONEERS

The numismatic trade has been around for centuries and arose as a sideline of goldsmiths and bankers. Spink & Son claimed to have been established in 1722, as their billhead of 1897 illustrates, but when historians were researching the firm's history for its bicentenary they discovered to their astonishment that it had actually been in existence since the Restoration of Charles II in 1660. William S. Lincoln of New Oxford Street was one of the leading dealers at the turn of the century, trading in postage stamps and crests as well as coins and medals. He was a prolific publisher of handbooks and monographs from which this advertisement of 1897 was taken. In an era before photographic illustrations were possible, reproductions of coins appeared as line drawings and in many cases these were much clearer than the actual photographs which later superseded them! By the nineteenth century London had become the centre of the world coin trade, and to this day it remains the headquarters of the leading auctioneers in this field, Sotheby's, Christie's, Glendining's and Spink's. The montage of coins, medals and decorations, including such rarities as the Japanese Oban (large oval gold coin) and the holey dollar of Australia (below the auctioneer's gavel) is typical of a recent Glendining's general sale.

Grades for Old Coins

Below VF coins are not really worth considering unless they are scarce in any case. Dealers do not usually handle modern items in the lower grades (unless they are rare); however, the following definitions may be useful for consideration where older material is concerned:

Fine (F) describes a coin in worn condition, although to the uninitiated it may seem a perfectly good specimen. Closer examination, however, will reveal that the higher points of the surface are worn smooth and the lettering has become thicker and coarser through constant handling.

Very Good (VG) is a euphemism that, like modern coinage, has become so debased that it now means rather bad! On such a coin only a small fraction of the finer detail would have survived while the portions in high relief, as well as the lettering, would be quite blurred.

Good (G) now means the exact opposite. A coin in this condition would be worn smooth all over. The date would be just readable and no more, and for this reason collectors will occasionally keep a coin in such bad condition when a particular year is scarce. Below this grade come **Fair, Mediocre** and **Poor**, terms that have become so abused in practice as to be virtually synonymous, although **Poor** usually refers to coins that are damaged as well as worn, either clipped or pierced. Coins have frequently been converted into jewellery, hence the piercing, but almost as bad are coins showing traces of solder where they have been mounted in rings or brooches; such blemishes detract from their numismatic value. Modern coins have to endure far more than their predecessors. Being passed from hand to hand is bad enough, but constant passage through parking meters and slot machines takes a heavy toll on coins.

Below: Ships have long been a popular coin theme, examples dating back to Greek and Roman coinage. Modern coins depicting ships are shown from the Cook Islands, South Africa, Brazil, the Isle of Man and Singapore.

Fine Distinctions

The grades listed above do not in themselves permit of the subtle, almost imperceptible, shading from one into the others, so it is sometimes necessary to modify them. Thus between FDC and EF one might find 'nearly FDC' and 'Good EF', while in the US collectors use such expressions as 'About Uncirculated' (AU) and 'EF plus'. Where one side is better than the other an oblique stroke between two grades (eg F/VF) indicates that the obverse is Fine while the reverse is Very Fine. The importance of mastering the meanings of these grades cannot be overemphasized. It is only human nature to overestimate the condition of coins, and dealers spend a large part of their time in turning away optimists who want to sell Very Good specimens in the mistaken belief that they are Extremely Fine.

'Slabbing'

Many of the trends in coin collecting have their origins in the US and the principles of 'slabbing' are now widely employed. Basically, this entails the precise grading of coins by an accredited dealer who then 'slabs' or encapsulates the coin in a small transparent folder that permits the details of the coin, including its grade, to be entered. The system, perfected by the American Numismatic Association, is now so precise as to have rendered the gradings used in Britain and Europe obsolete. American collectors now divide proofs into five distinct grades: **Proof-70** (Perfect Proof), **Proof-67** (Gem Proof), **Proof-65** (Choice Proof), **Proof-63** (Select Proof) and **Proof-60** (Proof). Uncirculated coins are graded into the same five categories, with MS (Mint State) prefixing a number: **MS-70** (Perfect), **MS-67** (Gem), **MS-65** (Choice), **MS-63** (Select) and **MS-60** (Uncirculated). Below 60, numbers 1 – 59 have been employed to indicate the various degrees of wear: Choice About Uncirculated (**AU-55**), About Uncirculated (**AU-50**), Choice Extremely Fine (**EF-45**), Extremely Fine (**EF-40**), Choice Very Fine (**VF-30**), Very Fine (**VF-20**), Fine (**F-12**), Very Good (**VG-8**), Good (**G-4**), About Good (**AG-4**) and Basal State (**BS-1**).

Above left and right: Many coins depict animals. Shown here are coins from Singapore (merlion), Norway (elkhound), Vatican (deer), Gibraltar (Barbary ape), the Isle of Man (tailless cat), Mauritius (sambar stag), Guernsey (dairy cow) and Cameroun (antelopes).

CARE OF COINS

There is no point in going to a great deal of trouble and expense in selecting the best coins you can afford, only to let them deteriorate in value by neglect and mishandling. Unless you give some thought to the proper care of your coins, your collection is unlikely to make a profit for you if and when you sell it. Housing your coins is the biggest problem of all, so it is important to give a lot of attention to this.

also versions designed as carrying cases, which are ideal for transporting coins. Coin-Safe of England have devised a drawer-stacking system with clear glass trays that fit into standard bookshelves. Lindner also produce coin boxes and capsules for individual items.

There are also various storage systems, such as Coindex, which operate on the principle of narrow drawers in which the coins are stored in envelopes of chemically-inert plastic. A strip across the top holds a little slip giving a brief description, catalogue number and the price of each coin. Kwikseal of the US produce cards with a plastic window; these cards are especially popular for slabbing coins. The traditional method used by many collectors was to house coins in small, air-dried manila envelopes that could be stored in narrow wooden or stout card boxes – knife-boxes were highly regarded as being the right width and depth. One Australian museum I visited recently kept its coins in manila envelopes stored in plastic lunch-boxes, which seemed to do the job pretty well.

Below: A typical coin cabinet. The close-fitting double doors keep out dust and atmospheric pollution. The shallow drawers contain trays drilled out in holes of various sizes to accommodate the appropriate coins. Note the circular white discs or 'tickets' on which collectors note the salient details, such as date and place of purchase and the price paid, as well as points of interest concerning the coins themselves.

Coins are best stored at average room temperature and humidity, so it is advisable to place small bags of silica gel crystals in the cabinets or boxes to combat atmospheric moisture. These crystals are hygroscopic and absorb water from the atmosphere, turning from blue to pink in the process. The silica gel crystals can be recycled quickly by drying them out in an oven.

Storage

The ideal, but admittedly the most expensive, method is the coin cabinet, constructed of air-dried mahogany, walnut or rosewood (*never* oak, cedar or any highly resinous timber likely to cause chemical tarnish). These cabinets have banks of shallow drawers containing trays made of the same wood, with half-drilled holes of various sizes to cater for the different denominations of coins. They are handsome pieces of furniture but, being largely handmade, tend to be very expensive. An excellent compromise is provided by firms such as Lindner of Germany and Abafil of Italy, who manufacture coin trays in durable, felt-lined materials with shallow compartments to suit various sizes of coin. These trays interlock so that they build up into a cabinet of the desired size, and there are

Right: Coin cases have become immensely popular in recent years and provide the ideal method of transporting coins as well as keeping them in good condition. Usually constructed of stout plastic, the trays are cloth-lined for maximum protection.

The Drawbacks of Coin Albums

When coin collecting became a popular hobby in the 1960s, several firms marketed ranges of coin albums. They had clear plastic sleeves divided into tiny compartments of various sizes and had the merit of being cheap and taking up little room, as several albums could be stored upright on a bookshelf. They had several drawbacks, however, not the least being the tendency of the pages to sag with the weight of the coins, or even, in extreme cases, to pull away from the pegs or rings holding them to the spine. They required very careful handling as the coins could easily fall out of the top row as the pages were turned. The more expensive albums had little flaps that folded over the top of the coin to overcome this problem. Arguably the worst aspect of these albums was the use of polyvinyl chloride (PVC) in the construction of the sleeves. Collectors soon discovered that this reacted chemically with their coins, especially those made of silver, causing a rather disgusting yellow slime to adhere to the coins' surface. This happened to me, and it took a considerable amount of time

Right: Coins may be carefully handled by the rim between forefinger and thumb.

and heartache before I was able to put the matter right.

Cleaning coins is something that should never be undertaken lightly; indeed, it is better not to attempt it than risk irreparable damage. In this case, however, immersion in lukewarm water with a small quantity of mild detergent and a great deal of patient and delicate wiping with cottonwool swabs eventually restored the coins to their original condition. After careful drying, they were rehoused in more conventional coin trays. There are still coin albums on the market, but as long as their pages and sleeves are of chemically-inert plastic materials, such as polyethylene, you should not encounter any problems.

CLEANING COINS

This is like matrimony – it should not be embarked on lightly. Indeed, the advice given by the magazine *Punch* in regard to marriage is equally sound in this case – don't do it! It is far better to have a dirty coin than an irretrievably damaged one. Every dealer has horror stories of handling coins that previous owners have cleaned, to their detriment. The worst example I ever

BRANCHING OUT IN COLLECTING

Sooner or later you will find that if you are going to make any headway with your hobby you will have to specialize. To a large extent your choice of subject will depend on the amount of money you have available to spend on coins, but personal preferences are also important and a surprising range of different aspects of numismatics can be tailored to suit your tastes and pocket. One area for specialization would be the early

Coins should always be handled with care, by holding the rims between forefinger and thumb. The acids and oils secreted by the fingers can leave indelible fingerprints on coins, so it is better to wear a pair of fine silk or cotton gloves while handling coins. Plastic tongs are available but it takes some practice to use them with dexterity and there is always the risk that you might accidentally drop a coin on the table or floor, with disastrous results.

coins of the West Indies. The romance of pirates, buccaneers and swashbuckling on the Spanish Main is reflected in the array of coins shown here. Many coins from Europe circulated in the Caribbean, but were countermarked with new values and insignia to denote local usage. Small change was created in two ways. You could either cut a large coin into smaller pieces such as halves, quarters and tiny segments, or you could punch out the centre and countermark both the central plug and the outer ring for use as coins of different denominations. A long bit was 15 cents and a short bit 10 cents, and from these curious practices came the American expression 'two bits' (25 cents) and even the bit *which was the official unit of currency in the Danish West Indies from 1904 to 1917.*

saw was a display of coins found by a metal detectorist who 'improved' his finds by abrading them in the kind of rotary drum used by lapidaries to polish gemstones. If you really must remove the dirt and grease from coins, it is advisable to practise on some coins that have no value.

Warm water containing a mild detergent will work wonders in removing surface dirt and grease from most coins, but silver is best washed in a decinormal solution of ammonia and warm water, while gold coins can be cleaned with dilute citric acid (such as lemon juice). Copper or bronze coins present more of a problem, but patches of verdigris can usually be removed by careful washing in a 20 per cent solution of sodium sesquicarbonate. Wartime coins made of tin, zinc, iron or steel can be cleaned in a 5 per cent solution of caustic soda containing some aluminium or zinc foil or filings, but they must be rinsed afterwards in clean water and carefully dried. Cotton buds are ideal for gently prising dirt out of coin legends. Soft brushes (with animal bristles – *never* nylon or other artificial fibres) designed for cleaning silver are most suitable for gently cleaning coins.

Coins recovered from soil or the sea bed present special problems, due to chemical reaction between the metals and the salts in the earth or sea water. In such cases, the best advice is to take them to the nearest museum and let the experts decide what can or should be done.

Polishing: A Warning

If cleaning should only be approached with the greatest trepidation, polishing is definitely *out!* Beginners sometimes fall into the appalling error of thinking that a smart rub with Brasso might improve the appearance of their coins. Short of actually punching a hole through it, I cannot imagine a more destructive act. Polishing a coin may improve its superficial appearance for a few days, but such abrasive action will destroy the patina and reduce the fineness of the high points of its surface. Even if a coin is only polished once, it will never be quite the same again, and an expert can tell this a mile off.

The Early Coins

Opposite: Different forms of money through the ages, from barter to credit card: trading a basket of grain for sheep, known as direct barter, gave way to indirect barter in which fixed values were expressed in objects such as strings of cowrie shells. Gold dust survived as a form of money in California and Tierra del Fuego till the late nineteenth century. Circular discs of precious metal with a recognizable emblem came into use in Asia Minor c.650 BC, the ancestor of our modern coins. Paper money was invented in China (thirteenth century), but the first European country to use banknotes was Sweden (1661). Cheques followed soon afterwards, but plastic credit cards did not develop till the late 1950s.

Nowadays we hear so much about the cashless society. Three-quarters of a century ago most transactions were made in coin, but the First World War replaced gold with paper money in general circulation. Now, the services offered by banks have become much more sophisticated; at one end of the scale we can obtain banknotes from a dispenser merely by punching a few keys, and at the other payment for goods and services can be made by direct debit. Computers and improved electronic communication systems have combined to make the spending of money easier than ever; all we need is a piece of plastic and we can travel the world without having to bother with different forms of currency.

Throughout the history of the civilized world wealth has taken many forms, from herds of cattle to tracts of land, from bars of gold stored in bank vaults to the figures at the bottom of your bank statement, from the bonds that denote the indebtedness of governments to their subjects to the certificates indicating a person's shareholding in public companies and private ventures. But none of these will buy you an ice cream or a loaf of bread. It is in the everyday business of life that coins come into their own.

Barter

Coins as we know them today have been around for almost 3,000 years. Long before that, and right down to the present time in the more remote and uncivilized regions of the world, money took the form of various objects on which a value was placed. The old civilizations of the Mediterranean basin were pastoral and their wealth lay in flocks of sheep and herds of cattle. Animals, meat and hides were used for barter or payment in kind and this is reflected in many of the words pertaining to money that are used to this day. From the Latin word *pecus*, meaning a herd, we get the word 'pecuniary'. The Greek word for a cow-hide was *talanton* and originally these skins were bartered. Later on, large pieces of copper shaped like cow-hides were substituted. These were far too cumbersome for general use, but the Greeks devised a ratio between copper and the precious metals (gold and

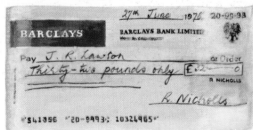

silver), so that 'talent' came to mean a specific weight of gold or silver and thence a monetary value. From another word for cow-hide, *byrsa*, we get the words 'purse' and 'bourse', respectively meaning a receptacle for money and a place where money changes hands. The word 'salary' comes from the salt, *sal*, paid to Roman soldiers as wages, while 'stipend' is derived from *stips* (a gift) and *pendere* (to weigh out). The Latin word *pondus*, meaning a weight, has given English words such as 'ponder' (to weigh up) and 'ponderous' (heavy), as well as 'pound' which can be a unit of weight (lb) or a unit of currency (£). The pound sign, which is actually a capital L with a stroke through it, comes from the Latin word *libra*, denoting a specific weight of one pound. A pound of silver in Roman and medieval times was used in reckoning large transactions, and has given us the units of currency used in many countries, such as the *livre* (France) and the *lira* (Italy, Turkey and Israel).

'SOILED' MONEY

Agricultural produce has also been used as money. Until the 1950s the inhabitants of Tristan da Cunha, a tiny island in the middle of the Atlantic Ocean, used potatoes as currency, two being worth a penny. The Arabs favoured beans (qirat), from which we get the word 'carat' (or 'karat' in the US), which nowadays is used both for a unit of weight in precious stones (200 mg) or a unit of fineness for gold, equal to 1/24th part of pure gold in an alloy. Cowrie shells, Cypraea moneta, were employed as small change in many parts of Asia and Africa until quite recently, at the rate of 200 to the Indian rupee. The slang expression 'to shell out' is said to derive from this.

Above: *Pu* money of China consisted of cast-bronze pieces imitating the spades, knives and hoes which had originally been bartered. These bronze pieces were used as currency from the seventh century BC.

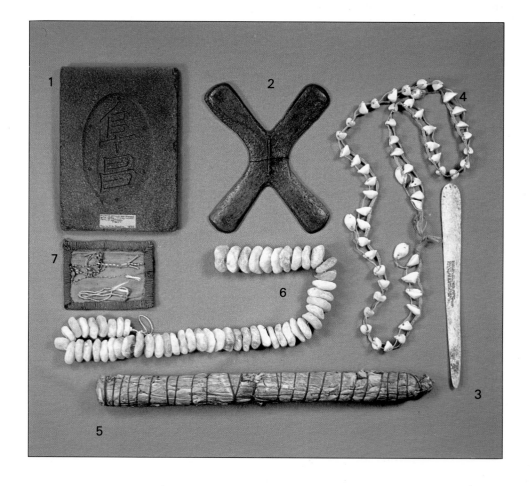

Right: Primitive money was used in many parts of the world until fairly recent times. 1. Tibetan machine press and dried tea brick; 2. copper cross from Katanga, Zaire; 3. potuma (dolphin's jawbone) from Marshall Bennett Island, Central Pacific; 4. shell money, New Guinea; 5. Ba Bunda salt packet; 6. quartz pebbles, West Africa; and 7. shell beads used as both jewellery and money.

From Objects to Coins

Shell discs, wampum, glass beads, the feathers of exotic birds, the teeth of sharks and walrus, and even enormous stone cartwheels have been used as money in many parts of the world. In China and other parts of Asia, implements and utensils made of bronze were traded and exchanged for centuries before it became customary to substitute small pieces of bronze fashioned into miniature representations of these articles. Bronze, which has given its name to an entire phase in the development of mankind, is an alloy of copper and tin.

Copper is probably the oldest metal to be used as money. Ironically, the word is derived from the Greek word *copros* (dung), but it gave the island of Cyprus its name, for copper was mined there 5,000 years ago. Alloyed with the tin found in Cornwall, it produced a hard and durable metal. Small bronze axes, known as celts, were used as money in Gaul and Britain. The earliest coinage used by the Romans consisted of heavy lumps known as *aes rude* (rough bronze). In Africa, copper crosses (Katanga) and rings known as manillas (Nigeria) were widely used as currency until the present century. In China, small discs of copper or bronze, with a square hole in the middle, began to evolve as coins long before the Christian era. The type was eventually fixed in AD 620 and remained current till the 1920s, making the Chinese *cash* the world's longest-running coin. Individual *cash* had very little value so hundreds or thousands of them, strung together, were required for large transactions. In Sweden copper was the principal monetary medium from 1644 until 1768 and resulted in the world's heaviest and most cumbersome coins, including the massive 10-daler plates which measured 35.5 × 61 cm (14 × 24 in) and weighed over 20 kg (44 lb). Significantly, China and Sweden were the first countries in the world to introduce paper money as a substitute for coins.

In other parts of the world, iron was more readily available, and this endured until the present century in the little winged rods known as *kissi* pennies in West Africa. In ancient Britain, crude ingots and bars of

Above: Chinese cast bronze *li* (or *cash*) from China (left) and 200 *mon* from Japan (right).

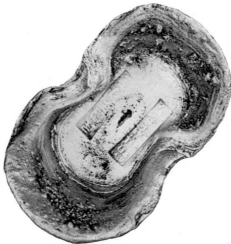

Among the strangest forms of primitive money is the *Fe* or stone money from Yap in the Marshall Islands (above right). Sycee silver from China bears marks showing that it had a value of 50 taels (below left). The gold *Oban* of Japan had a distinctive crenellated surface and in addition to the countermarks it bore the mintmaster's name in Indian ink.

iron were used as money, while iron rods or spits formed the small change of the Greeks. The Greek word for a spit or dart was *belos* and from this came the word *obol* meaning a small coin. From the verb *drassomai* (to grasp) came the word *drachma* which meant a handful (of spits) but later came to mean a unit of weight or a small silver coin. Gradually metal came to be equated with money. We can see this in such expressions as gold, silver, brass, tin and 'coppers' to indicate money in general or small change in particular. This is more obvious in other languages, such as French, where *argent* means 'money' as well as silver.

Merchants' Marks

Metals as exchange media were well established in ancient Greece at least 1,000 years before the Christian era. The Greeks even had a well-defined ratio of one metal in terms of others, so that a piece of gold was worth 13 pieces of silver of the same weight, or 3,000 pieces of copper. Gold in a relatively pure state was not as popular or practical as its alloy with silver, known as electrum or pale gold. At first, merchants had to weigh out each piece every time a transaction took place. This was time-consuming, so eventually merchants came to accept pieces of metal bearing a mark that was recognized as a guarantee of weight and purity. Initially such a mark took the form of a personal stamp, struck on the lump of metal with a broken nail whose jagged end would leave a distinctive impression. From this developed the chopmarks that Chinese traders applied until recent times to silver coins imported from Europe and America, as well as the medieval coins of India whose designs were made up entirely of patterns of elaborate countermarks. The silver pieces of Thailand, known as bullet money because of their distinctive shape, had devices stamped on them in the same way until 1880.

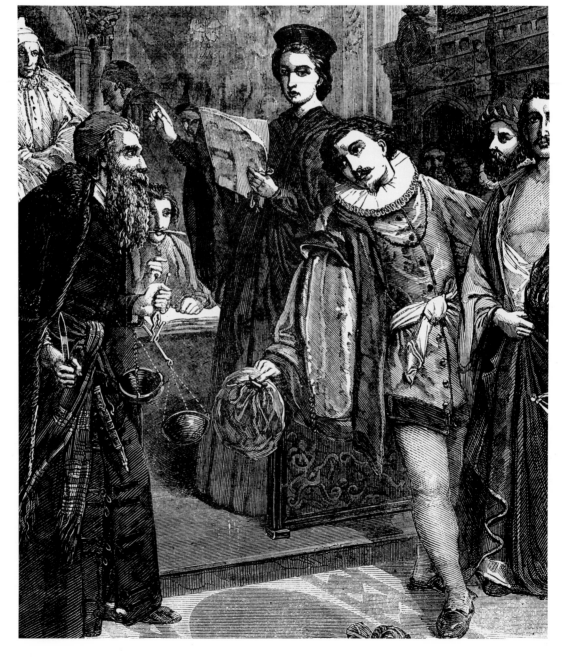

Right: A scene from Shakespeare's *Merchant of Venice*. By the end of the fifteenth century, the merchants of northern Italy had become so powerful that they were able to set up independent city states, such as Florence, Milan and Venice. These city states were ruled by merchant princes who controlled the trade of the Mediterranean and the Levant, just as the Hanseatic League controlled the Baltic and North Sea trade. They were responsible for many innovations in European coinage, from the florins of Florence (1252) to the sequins and ducats of Venice and the testoons of Milan (1474), widely copied all over Europe.

In Europe and the Middle East, however, the mark of the individual merchant developed into a single device that eventually occupied the whole of one side. At the same time, the crude lumps of metal became rounder and flatter, because of the process whereby the mark was applied. By 630 BC the crude nail mark had developed into a recognizable motif. This was the head of a lion, the badge of the Mermnad dynasty that ruled over Lydia in Asia Minor (modern Turkey). The device was engraved on the face of an iron anvil. On this, using a pair of tongs, a lump of electrum, that had been heated up to make it soft and malleable, was carefully laid. This was struck by a hammer with such force that the lump was squeezed flat and picked up an impression of the design. This side is known as the obverse of a coin (or 'heads' in everyday terms).

'Heads and Tails'

At first the reverse (or 'tails') was left blank and such coins are said to be uniface (one-sided). Gradually it became the custom to engrave a mark on the hammerhead, which produced a simple, geometric pattern on the other side of the coin. As the face of the hammer suffered considerable wear in the striking process, the next stage was to engrave a device on a piece of iron that was held over the lump of silver or gold and then took the blow from the hammer.

In this manner the system of coining irons for the obverse and reverse was developed. The reverse still took the brunt of the hammer-blows and thus wore out more quickly, so the more important and enduring motif was engraved on the obverse die, while the less important and more ephemeral details appeared on the reverse die. The obverse dies that have survived from Roman and medieval times generally have a large spike on the back. This was driven into an immense block of wood that took the place of the anvil. The reverse die, on the other hand, had a flattened back to take the hammer-blow. At first the reverse consisted of a simple incuse geometric mark (incuse means cut into the surface). Such a mark may be found on the early coins of Aegina. More elaborate incuse patterns graced the coins of Macedon, while Cretan coins, appropriately, showed the famous labyrinth of King Minos.

From this it was only a short step to making the reverse as elaborate as the obverse. The earliest coins of this type date from the middle of the sixth century BC and were minted in Athens. The obverse bore a profile of the goddess Athena while the reverse depicted an owl (this, as classical scholars would say, was her 'attribute', a symbol of wisdom). This established a precedent that was followed by many of the Greek city-states: a portrait of a deity on the obverse and a pictorial emblem on the reverse. This pattern is widely used on coins to the present day, hence the effigy of Queen Elizabeth on the obverse of British 10p coins and the lion on the reverse, or the profile of George Washington, linked to the American eagle on the quarter dollar of the US.

Above: Most popular of the trade coins in ancient Greece were the 'owls' of Athens, silver tetradrachms which earned their nickname from the owl on the reverse. The example (left) was one of the first coins to bear an inscription – *Athe*. The dekadrachm or 10 drachmae piece (right) showed an owl with wings spread.

Below: USA: quarter-dollar reverse showing the American bald eagle perched on the fasces or bundle of rods. The obverse of this coin portrays George Washington, the first president and known as 'the Father of his Country'.

By the fourth century BC the whole of the civilized world used coins, each kingdom, principality and city-state having its own distinctive series. Nowadays there are not many countries without their own coins and none that does not use coins in one form or another.

How Coins are Made

There are two methods of producing coins. The normal method is to strike a piece of metal that has been specially prepared for the purpose, but an alternative method has sometimes been used in the past. This entails heating metal until it is in a molten state and then pouring it into a mould. Coins produced by this method are said to be 'cast'.

CAST COINS

The earliest coins of ancient Rome, the *aes rude*, and their successors, the *aes grave* (heavy bronze), were cast in moulds bearing the shape or impression of the required images. Casting was the technique used in China to produce the *pu, shu* and *tao* bronze pieces. The *chi 'en*, or *cash*, were also cast, often in clusters or 'trees' in which individual coins were linked by the branches created by the molten metal running through the channels of the mould. Complete trees are rare and much sought after, as the coins were usually broken off as required. One can generally recognize a cast coin by the marks on the edge showing where the runnel has been broken off, or by the file marks where attempts have been made to smooth this away.

Japan's cast coinage commenced in AD 708 and followed the pattern of the Chinese *cash*. Copper, bronze, brass or iron, *mon*, continued to be used until 1870. In addition, there were *Cho Gin* (literally 'long silver') or elliptical ingots marked with chops, and small, thin, rectangular pieces such as the *chibu Gin* and the *Nibu Kin*, in silver and gold respectively. The most spectacular cast coins were the large, thin plates with rounded corners and textured surfaces, stamped with chops and inscribed with characters painted in Indian ink. They were cast in an alloy of gold and silver and known as *Koban, Goryoban* and *Oban*, tariffed at 1, 5 and 10 *ryo* respectively. Korea used cast coins like Chinese *cash* from 1633 'till 1891, while some of the Malay states continued this system until 1895. Burma and Indochina graduated to circular coins in the nineteenth century under British and French influence, but previously used cast bronze pieces in the shape of hats, cannon and animal figures. Elsewhere, cast coins were only fleetingly used, usually in times of emergency. In 1826, the besieged Spanish garrison in the Chiloé archipelago cast copies of the Potosí 8 reales of 1822. At Terceira in the Azores, 20, 40 and 80 reis were cast from gun metal in 1829 in the name of the exiled Queen Maria II. During the Mexican revolution Rafael Buelna issued cast pesos at Sinaloa in June 1913. Oddly enough, the first true coins of the Isle of Man (1709) were cast in a local foundry.

Below: Isle of Man halfpenny of 1709, a rare example of a European cast coin.

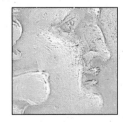

THE DIE METHOD

The usual method of producing a coin, however, was to impress the image from a die, or pair of dies, on a piece of metal by means of a hammer blow. This is essentially the method in use to the present day, although, of course, the process has been considerably refined over the centuries. The piece of metal (known as a blank, flan or planchet) was originally cast in a shallow mould. The Spaniards in Latin America, from Mexico City (1600) to Argentina (1824), cast raw silver into bars, slices of which then became the blanks for coins crudely clipped to the right weight, heated up and hammered between two dies. Only those struck at Lima in 1688 were reasonably well made; the rest are really vile. These crude versions of the famous pieces of eight are known as cobs, from the Spanish *cobo de barra* (cut from a bar).

The method developed in Europe in the Middle Ages was to hammer out a sheet of gold or silver to the required thickness and then cut out a circular blank with stout shears. The blanks were then trimmed and filed to the exact weight, the filings being carefully saved and recycled. The blanks were struck by hand, using a technique that varied little from the pre-Christian era to the sixteenth century. The Greeks attained

considerable skill in the cutting of coin dies and the resulting coins are masterpieces in miniature. The most outstanding feature of Greek coins is their comparatively high obverse relief. Many of the portraits found on silver tetradrachms of the fourth and fifth centuries BC are very realistic and almost three-dimensional. Roman coins, on the other hand, are generally flatter, with greater emphasis on the lettering of the legend (the inscription running round the circumference).

Like so much else, the art of coining suffered grievously during the Dark Ages. The techniques of intaglio gem-engraving, practised by the Greeks and Romans, virtually disappeared. Medieval European coins made little attempt at realistic portraiture. Effigies became stereotyped and stylized to the point of caricature. The lines of portraits, symbols and inscriptions were, in fact, punched into the dies by means of various chisels, each of which produced a dot, squiggle or wedge-shaped line. It was not until the Renaissance in the fifteenth century that the design and engraving of dies attained the standard lost by Rome more than a thousand years earlier. From then until the early nineteenth century, the quality of coin design rested very largely on the skill and craftsmanship of the engraver who had the job of cutting the

Below: The silver tetradrachms of the ancient Greek world were relatively thick and sculpted in high relief. Alexander the Great struck coins at Alexandria (c.326–318 BC) alluding to his mythical ancestry. The obverse showed the legendary hero Hercules, while the reverse depicted Zeus holding an eagle. After Alexander's death, however, he was deified, hence the horn of Ammon on his temple.

motifs and lettering into the dies. Each die was engraved separately so that many subtle differences occurred and the resulting coins of a single issue might vary quite considerably.

In the 1820s, however, a number of technical advances were made. Collas of Paris invented a reducing machine that did away with the need for hand-engraving, and chemical processes for hardening steel revolutionized the manufacture of dies.

Modern Coin Design

In the present day, the design of a coin begins with an artist producing a sketch in pen and ink, based on picture research to ensure that every detail of the design is accurate. A great deal of thought and planning goes into this initial stage, involving many hours of high-level discussion between the mint and officials of the country concerned and it is then that the practicality of the various motifs is examined in detail. At this point, experts in various fields, from art historians and museum curators to botanists and ichthyologists, may be consulted to ensure that the proposed design is absolutely accurate. The basis for the pictorial element on coins may come from a photograph, a painting or a piece of sculpture, but it has to be translated into a preliminary drawing integrated into the shape of the eventual coin, together with lettering, value and symbolic elements. From this is assembled a finished design that is submitted to the appropriate government body for approval. In the case of coins intended for use in the UK and many Commonwealth countries, Queen Elizabeth herself must be consulted because her effigy appears on the obverse.

Sculpting

Once the concept of the design has been approved, it progresses from the drawing board to the sculptor's table. An enlarged maquette is fashioned in Plasticine or modelling clay. When this is complete down to the last detail, plaster casts are taken from it. Many hours may be spent working over the plaster before the image is judged to be perfect. At this stage the sculptor can still make minor changes and

improvements using fine dental drills. The master cast, given a positive impression, is then made into a matrix of hard chrome and nickel and fitted to the cutting machine. Here the image is cut on a hub or master die by a steel cutter working in unison with a stylus that moves slowly over the hardened matrix, rather like the needle of a record-player, but from the centre to the outer edge. This process takes up to 72 hours. By means of a reducing machine, the design is transferred to a hub of the correct dimensions of the eventual coin. Completed hubs are examined painstakingly through a high-powered magnifier.

Hubbing

The next stage, known as hubbing, transfers the image from the hub to the working die. A negative impression is picked up on the die, using a 400-tonne press to apply pressure to the blank die. After turning and milling, the soft steel die is hardened chemically and physically by heating it in a special, temperature-controlled salt bath for about 12 hours, and is then quenched in a special solution. This gives the die its unique hardness and durable qualities needed for the high pressures and for the intense clarity required in the coining process. After hardening, the dies are ground and polished by hand to a mirror-like finish, using ground diamonds. They are now ready for coining.

Above: The noted medallist Leslie Lindsay sculpting the master design for a coin. The artist works in modelling clay from a pen and ink drawing.

Below: The actual dies used by the German troops in East Africa to produce emergency copper and brass 20 heller coins in 1916.

MECHANIZATION

The coining strip of the present day is a far cry from the old hammered gold and silver plates. This was, in fact, the first aspect of coin production to become mechanized. In 1551 a mint was established at the Moulin des Etuves on the Île de la Cité in Paris. This establishment took its name from the water-mill that provided the power to drive the machinery used to roll out the metal to a uniform thickness. Perfectly formed blanks were, in fact, the key to the success of an operation that continued to depend to a large extent on the age-old hammered techniques. A Huguenot refugee named Eloi Mestrell brought the new technology to England and produced the first milled coins of Queen Elizabeth from 1561 to 1571. The jealousy of the hammermen secured his dismissal, however, and he died on the gallows at Norwich where he was hanged in 1578 for counterfeiting.

Another Frenchman, Nicholas Briot, revived the notion of mechanically produced, perfectly shaped coins, first at the Paris mint and then, from 1625 until his death in 1646, in England, where he struck coins of great beauty and symmetry. The Civil War put an end to Briot's experiments. A further trial with rolling machinery was made by Pierre Blondeau at the Tower of London under the patronage of Oliver Cromwell from 1651 onwards. This work was still in an embryonic stage at the Restoration of 1660, but two years later milled coinage was widely released in England.

Nowadays the metal used in coins is supplied to a mint in enormous coiled strips that are cut into the required shapes or flans in blanking presses under a pressure of 50 tonnes per 6.45 sq cm (1 sq in). After cutting, the blanks are carefully checked for slivers and crescents of surplus metal and then passed through various annealing and blanching processes where they are degreased, cleaned, washed, dried and brought to a brilliant light lustre suitable for coining.

Coins intended for general circulation are nowadays produced on high-speed presses at a pressure of 180 tonnes per 6.45 sq cm. Presses for making coins were devised in the fifteenth century, soon after the invention of the printing press, and took two distinct forms. Donato Bramante (1444–1514) invented the screw press, which was first used to strike papal bulls (lead seals). The reverse die was brought down on the blank with enormous pressure by the rotation of a vertical screw, using a windlass operated by two men. This was a slow and time-consuming process, calling for great strength and dexterity. About the same time, however, a roller press, operating along the same lines as a clothes-mangle, was invented in Austria, and from 1566 onwards this was the standard coin press throughout the Holy Roman Empire. The dies fitted to this type of press were ovoid rather than circular to compensate for the curvature of the rollers. Presses of

Below: Obverse and reverse of the gold unite (20 shillings) produced by Nicholas Briot at the Tower of London in 1631–32 using machinery. This handsome coin was the forerunner of the milled coins which came into general use thirty years later.

MINTING IN THE MIDDLE AGES

Craftsmen at work in a medieval mint (above opposite). On the far left a worker cuts and trims the blanks from metal sheets using giant shears. In front of him a hammerman beats out a sheet of silver to a uniform thickness prior to blanking. On his left a master craftsman strikes the pile and trussel containing a blank while his assistant prepares a fresh blank. A basin of finished coins lies at his feet. In the background is the mintmaster checking the accounts, with a balance used in assaying and checking the blanks on his right.

this type were also adopted by the Segovia mint in 1586 and applied to Spanish coins.

The hand-operated roller and screw presses continued in use well into the nineteenth century. In 1786, the Scottish inventor and pioneer of steam-power, James Watt, teamed up with the Birmingham businessman Matthew Boulton to form the Soho Mint. This mint was the first in the world to produce coins on automatic presses operated by steam, the celebrated Cartwheel twopence of 1797 being one of the first of its products. Twelve years later the Royal Mint ordered steam presses in preparation for the reform of the coinage in 1816. These operated on the screw principle, but in 1818 Dietrich Uhlhorn of Düsseldorf invented the lever press and by the late nineteenth century this type was in universal use. Steam gave way to hydraulic power and latterly electricity.

MODERN MACHINERY

In modern high-speed presses the blanks are fed into the dial plates and pass through two check-points that determine thickness and diameter, before they reach the coining station. As it is struck, each flan is subjected to a security counter that gives the precise number of coins minted by that press. Theoretically, this prevents the accidental striking of a blank while another is still on the dial plate, but this still sometimes occurs. One coin will be overstruck on the other and the resulting mis-strikes are known to collectors as brockages. They may be recognized by partial or imperfect impressions or a slight doubling of the image. Conversely, should the mechanism fail to place a blank on the dial plate, the dies will strike each other. Not surprisingly,

this does them no good and produces clash marks that, in turn, will be impressed on any blanks subsequently struck.

After striking, the coins are check-weighed and examined for flaws and defects. After passing this examination, they are counted again in a numbering machine and hermetically sealed in bags before a final check-weighing. Test samples are taken at frequent intervals during the various stages to check by micrometer that the correct tolerances of diameter and thickness are being adhered to.

Coins that are manufactured nowadays must be struck to the highest precision because they are increasingly employed in all manner of slot machines, from parking meters and telephone boxes to automats and vending equipment whose acceptor-rejector mechanism is finely tuned to prevent the use of foreign coins.

What Coins are Made of

With a few notable exceptions, a coin is a piece of metal of a fixed weight and purity, struck by the authority of a government and employed as a circulating medium. In many countries (notably in Latin America) the weight and fineness is actually inscribed on precious metal coins, and this practice has been extended to many of the gold, silver and platinum bullion coins of recent times. A coin is a legal tender, which means that a law has been passed decreeing that it cannot be refused in payment of goods and services up to the value at which it circulates. It is strictly protected by law, which sometimes exacts very rigorous penalties on those who counterfeit or mutilate it (eg by clipping pieces off the rim).

> ### FORGERY
> *Counterfeiting, the forging and uttering of false coins, is one of the world's oldest professions; Aeginetan staters of the sixth century BC have been found to have a copper core plated with silver. In 1125, King Henry I had all the mint officials mutilated by cutting off their right hands as a penalty for counterfeiting coinage, while at other times, as well as in other countries, the counterfeiting of gold and silver coins was a capital offence. In the Isle of Man, however, forgers of even copper coins were liable to death by hanging.*

COINAGE METALS

The coinage of a country is usually divided into categories according to the metals or alloys used. In the past the principal coinage metals were gold, silver and bronze (or copper) for which collectors use the abbreviations AV, AR and AE (from the Latin words *aurum*, *argentum* and *aes*. The alloy of gold and silver, known as pale gold or electrum, has already been mentioned. In historic times gold coins were usually minted in almost pure metal, of 23.5 carats fine. The modern equivalent is 'three nines' gold (999 in 1000 parts) and these numerals may be found on such modern bullion coins as the Canadian maple leaf. In 1984, however, the Royal Canadian Mint succeeded in refining gold to .9999 pure, and began striking maple leaves with the 'four nines' inscription. The drawback of pure gold is its softness. In 1526, King Henry VIII debased his gold by introducing the crown of the double rose, struck to only 22 carat (.917) fineness. Later monarchs operated a dual system of 'fine' gold (mainly for presentation pieces) and 'crown' gold (for everyday circulation). This continued until the outbreak of the Civil War in 1642 but thereafter only crown gold was used. British gold was traditionally alloyed with copper – hence its reddish lustre. In other countries gold is often alloyed with silver, resulting in a yellower colour.

Left: The angel, introduced by King Edward IV in 1465, was required when the previous gold coin, the noble, was raised in value to 8s 4d. Because a coin worth a third of a pound was needed, the angel was issued to fill the gap. It took its name from the figure of the Archangel Michael slaying the serpent, a personification of the triumph of good over evil. The reverse showed a heraldic shield on the side of a ship, surmounted by a large cross. Because of the religious subjects on this coin it rapidly acquired a reputation as a talisman or lucky piece and was later used by successive monarchs in the ceremony of touching for the King's Evil. Angels were last minted by Charles I shortly before the outbreak of the English Civil War in 1642.

Silver

In its virtually pure state silver is likewise too soft for practical durability, yet this was the fineness used for the *pesos a ocho reales*, the famous 'pieces of eight' produced in such abundance by the Latin American mints. In medieval Europe the purest silver obtainable was 23/24 or .958 fine, variously known in Germany and France as *Königsilber* or *Argent le Roi* (king silver), but it was rarely used for coins. In England from Anglo-Saxon times, 92.5 per cent silver was alloyed with 7.5 per cent copper. This was the mixture used for the 'easterlings', as silver pennies were commonly known, and from this developed the term 'sterling', originally denoting the English coinage standard but ultimately becoming a by-word for quality. The impecunious Henry VIII progressively debased his silver coinage, first to .750, then to .500 and finally to .333 fineness. Any alloy containing less than 50 per cent silver is known as billon. Henry's billon coins contained so much copper that the reddish metal showed as soon as the coins began to wear. As the most prominent feature of his full-face portrait was the first part of the surface to betray its true nature, these coins were soon nicknamed 'Coppernoses'. Incredibly, some countries issued silver coins of an even lower quality. Black billon, otherwise known in Latin as *argentum nigrum* or white copper *moneta argentosa,* contained 75 per cent copper and 25 per cent silver and was used in the Netherlands. The record for the poorest quality is held by Mexico whose pesos of 1957–67 were a mere .100 fine!

Platinum

Platinum was used for Russian 3, 6 and 12 rouble coins in 1826–45 but was never as popular as gold. At one time it was much cheaper than gold and because of its high specific gravity it was much favoured by counterfeiters who gave their products a plating of the yellow metal. When industrial uses for platinum were discovered, however, its value rocketed and ever since it has tended to trade at a handsome premium over gold. A ban on modern gold coins in the 1960s, by Britain's Labour government, induced several countries, such as Sierra Leone and Tonga, to produce coins in platinum aimed at investors seeking a hedge against inflation and in 1983 the Isle of Man launched the noble as the world's first bullion coin in this metal. Since 1966, several countries have struck coins in palladium, a dense white metal of the platinum group.

Copper

Copper and the alloys derived from it have been widely used for subsidiary coinage since classical times. The Romans favoured a brassy alloy known as orichalcum for their dupondii and sestertii. Collectors, however, use the term 'brass' indiscriminately to describe the whole range of Roman copper coinage. Copper, as a base metal, went out of favour in Western Europe, although it continued in the Byzantine Empire and, of course, formed the basis of currency in the Far East. It re-emerged as a coinage metal in Europe in the sixteenth century. In England, successive governments stuck rigidly

Below: UK: farthings of Queen Victoria in copper (left) and bronze (right).

to silver for even the smallest values. When the public demanded copper farthings for small change, King James I granted a licence in 1613 to Lord Harrington, and later to the Duke of Lennox, to mint such coins in copper. It was not until 1672 that the government bowed to economic pressure and authorized base metal halfpence and farthings. Copper was used at first but tin farthings were substituted in 1684 in a bid to help the ailing Cornish tin industry. Tin is not a satisfactory metal for coinage because it corrodes rapidly, but when alloyed with copper it produces bronze. Pure copper was used for British subsidiary coinage until 1860 when bronze was substituted. This alloy also contains some zinc or lead and today it is widely used for minor coins all over the world.

Other alloys of copper have been used from time to time. Bath metal is a pale brass containing a high proportion of zinc to copper; this was used by William Wood of Bath to produce Irish halfpence and the Rosa Americana coinage for the American colonies (1722–4), and by his successors to strike pennies for the Isle of Man in 1734. Bell metal (78 per cent copper and 22 per cent tin) is a type of bronze used for casting bells. It was used during the French Revolution for 1 and 2 sou coins made from metal obtained by melting down the church bells. Gunmetal (90 per cent copper and 10 per cent tin), obtained from old cannon, was used for Irish coins struck by James II in 1689–90. History repeated itself almost a century later when coins of Moldo-Walachia were struck at Sadogoura from captured Turkish guns.

Nickel

Nickel was mined in India and used for coins of Bactria as long ago as the third century BC, but it then languished in oblivion until the nineteenth century. It was revived in the US in 1856, when 12 parts of nickel were added to 88 parts of copper in the Flying Eagle cents (1856–8) and the first of the Indian Head cents (1859–64) before bronze was substituted. The nickel was just sufficient to impart a pale reddish colour to these coins. Belgium (1860) adopted a higher proportion of nickel (25 per cent) for 5, 10 and 20 centimes. Despite the high copper content, this alloy proved to be a tolerable substitute for silver and was subsequently adopted by the US for the 3 cents of 1865 and the 5 cents of 1866. The 3 cent coins were discontinued in 1889 but the 5 cent continues to this day and has long been known as a 'nickel'. Curiously enough, a shortage of nickel required for cartridge cases led to the replacement, in 1942–5, of the traditional cupro-nickel alloy by a mixture of 56 per cent copper, 35 per cent silver and 9 per cent manganese – a unique instance of precious metal replacing base metal due to the exigencies of war.

Switzerland (1879) introduced cupro-nickel for 5 and 10 rappen. Pure nickel, producing a brighter, more silvery appearance, was adopted for the 20 rappen of 1881, and this was the approach followed by Austria for the 10 and 20 heller of 1892. As a substitute for silver, pure nickel has since been used by many countries. Nickel alloyed with silver has been used by Switzerland and nickel alloyed with steel has been used in recent years by Afghanistan.

Top left: USA: the first 'nickel' 5 cent coin, actually an alloy of 75 per cent copper and 25 per cent nickel. Until 1965 this was the only nickel coin in circulation in the USA, hence the name 'nickel' given to 5 cent coins.

Top right: Netherlands: pure nickel gulden with the portrait of Queen Juliana on the obverse.

Iron

Iron has been used extensively over the past 150 years. It was used for the cast 20 *cash* Hsien Feng coins of Fukien and Chekiang (1851–61) as well as the Doosa-Seni coinage of Japan. Iron coins appeared in many different shapes in various parts of nineteenth-century Africa. It was adopted in Europe during the First World War, iron coins being issued by the Germans for use in the occupied Soviet Union. Norway and Denmark produced coins in varnished iron, while Sweden used nickel-plated iron in 1917. A form of stainless steel known as acmonital has been used in Italy since 1939. In 1940 both magnetic and non-magnetic steel was used, so collectors treat them as distinct varieties.

Top left: Italy: Acmonital (stainless steel) 100 lire.

Right: Zinc coins from Poland, Austria, Belgium and Denmark. The Polish 10 groszy was originally issued in cupro-nickel in 1923 and reissued in 1941–44 (with the 1923 date) in zinc during the German occupation.

Zinc

Zinc has a silvery appearance when newly minted, so it has been used as a substitute for precious metal, usually in times of war and financial crises, but it oxidizes to an unattractive dull blue-grey colour. Many states in Asia struck zinc coins in the nineteenth century, but it was first used in Europe in 1923–5 when Czechoslovakia issued 2 haleru coins. It was extensively used during and immediately after the Second World War, especially in the countries occupied by Nazi Germany. An alloy of copper and zinc is used for the 1, 2 and 5 jiao coins of the People's Republic of China, while a somewhat similar alloy, known as tombac, replaced nickel in the wartime coinage of Canada. A triple alloy of copper, nickel and zinc is now widely used in many countries, while zinc-coated steel replaced bronze in the US cents of 1943.

Tin

Tin was used for English farthings of 1684–92 and halfpence of 1685–92, as well as farthings issued by Antigua in 1836 but it corrodes badly. The only part of the world to use tin extensively was Malaya where many of the sultanates of the eighteenth and nineteenth centuries produced kepings and pitis in this metal. Tin alloyed with lead produces pewter, used in the provincial coinage of China, but otherwise confined to a few emergency issues, such as the coins struck during the siege of Prague in 1757. Potin is an alloy of 20 per cent silver mixed with copper, tin, zinc and lead. This may have been quite silvery when newly minted but such coins generally have a blackish grey colour. It was an alloy much favoured by the Celtic tribes in pre-Christian times, but, with a small amount of gold added, it was also used for tetradrachms struck at Alexandria. Lead in its more or less pure form was used by Frederick III of Denmark for several denominations minted about 1660. It was also fleetingly used in China and the East Indies, but the most noteworthy series of lead coins was that issued by the Andhra dynasty of India (100 BC–AD 200). It was also extensively used for tokens in seventeenth-century England (see Chapter 7).

Aluminium

Aluminium (or aluminum in North America) was something of a curiosity until its lightness, durability and resistance to corrosion made it popular in everything from pots and pans to the statue of Eros in Piccadilly Circus, London. As a coinage metal it made its debut in 1907 when it was used for tenth pennies issued by British West Africa. In the same year, cents and half cents of aluminium were issued in British East Africa. However, aluminium proved to be too light and insubstantial for the public's liking and in 1908 it was replaced by cupro-nickel. Several countries had emergency issues of aluminium tokens during the First World War. Germany released aluminium pfennigs in 1916–18 and 50 pfennig coins in 1919–22, while Romania struck 25 and 50 bani coins in 1921, but it was not until the Second World War that

Left: Aluminium coins from Poland, the People's Republic of China, Iceland and Cyprus.

Aluminium as a coinage metal was pioneered by the British West Africa tenth-penny (above) and the East Africa and Uganda Protectorate cent in 1907, but it was regarded as too light and insubstantial so the experiment was discontinued in 1908. Strangely enough, it was then replaced by cupronickel (below) although this alloy is more generally regarded as a silver substitute in coins of a comparatively high face value.

aluminium coins became widespread and since then aluminium has been used in many countries. As a rule, it has been confined to the very smallest coins, whose only reason for existence is to make up odd amounts in change, but in the German Democratic Republic the vast majority of the circulating coins, from the humble pfennig to the 2 mark piece, were struck in this cheap metal.

Alloyed with bronze, however, aluminium produces a heavier substance with a bright golden appearance. Oddly enough, this brass alloy was used for East Germany's 20 pfennig coins, in stark contrast to the rest of the series. It was first used by France for the Chamber of Commerce 50 centimes and the 1 and 2 francs of the 1920s and then retained for the government issues of these denominations until 1941 when it was replaced by aluminium. Germany's rentenpfennig and reichspfennig issues from 1923 onwards also made extensive use of this alloy until the outbreak of the Second World War.

Alloys

The vast majority of coins are struck from an alloy in which the component metals are mixed at the molten stage. In classical and medieval times, however, base metal coins were sometimes given a 'wash' of gold or silver to give them the appearance of precious metal, and there are numerous examples of coins of the present century that consist of one metal plated with another. Chrome-plated steel, for example, was used by France for the 5 centime coins of 1961–4 while the US used zinc-plated steel for the cents of 1943.

Coins have also been made of two different metals or alloys. The main blank is of one metal, usually the cheaper or baser component, but into this is set a plug or small disc of more expensive metal. English farthings of 1684–5 were made of tin, but their value was enhanced by a copper plug. About 1844 Joseph Moore of Birmingham devised a solution to the problem of copper coins whose intrinsic value was approximately the same as their circulating value. This had resulted in copper coins that were too cumbersome to be practical, so

Aluminium-bronze is now very popular on account of its bright golden colour. (Below) Vatican: 20 lire, Pope John Paul II, 1981. (Above) Mexico: 50 centavos, 1951.

CLAD COINS

Since the 1960s, many countries (notably the US and West Germany) have issued 'clad' coins as a means of preserving the traditional appearance of coins while reducing the precious metal content. Thus, a silver coin such as the quarter dollar could be issued with a core of copper in a thin sandwich of silver or nickel. You can recognize clad coins because the material of the inner core shows through at the edge.

Bimetallic coins: Joseph Moore's model penny (above) and a modern American transport token (below).

Moore struck small copper coins whose value was made up by having a tiny plug of silver in the centre. Though popular with the public, these 'model coins' were not adopted by the Royal Mint. In recent years, however, Italy has issued 200 lire coins with a steel outer ring and an aluminium bronze centre.

Non-metallic coins

During and immediately after the First World War, several European countries permitted the circulation of pasteboard tokens, which may be found in square, octagonal or circular shapes. From the American Civil War (1861–5) until the Spanish Civil War (1936–9) postage stamps encased or affixed to pasteboard discs were used in many countries during a shortage of small change. During the monetary crisis that overtook Germany immediately after the First World War, the Meissen potteries produced emergency coins made of porcelain or stoneware on behalf of several municipal authorities and chambers of commerce, for general circulation in 1921–2. Thailand had porcelain coinage during the nineteenth century; these pieces were originally produced as gambling tokens but during a shortage of small change they were pressed into service. In 1913 the Cocos (Keeling) Islands introduced a series of seven (5 cents to 5 rupees) coins made of a proto-plastic substance known as ivorine, intended for the use of workers on the coconut plantations. These were followed in 1968 by a series in coloured plastic (blue for the cent denominations and red for the rupee values) which remained current until 1977 when more orthodox coins of bronze, cupro-nickel, silver and gold were released.

Below: Wooden nickels are popular with collectors in the US where they are produced for all kinds of events of local and national importance. They are much larger than ordinary coins and have designs printed in colour on both sides. They enjoy limited validity, usually redeemable for cash, goods or services within a stated time. The idea arose during the Depression years when these tokens were issued to the unemployed and the needy and could be exchanged for food, clothing and accommodation.

All Shapes and Sizes

SHAPE

Although coins are usually circular in shape and fairly uniform in thickness, this is by no means standard and over the centuries there have been many variations, many of which are still collectable.

Curiosities

The earliest coins were irregular lumps of metal; so long as the weight and fineness were constant, the actual shape or thickness was not important, and later primitive coins have been globular (Lydia), bean-shaped (ancient Persia) or bullet-shaped (Thailand). The larins of the Persian Gulf states and the Maldive Islands took the form of thin bars of silver often bent at one end in the shape of a fish-hook, and stamped with the denomination, whereas the sycee currency of the Far East in the nineteenth and early twentieth centuries was boat-shaped. The oban and koban coinage of Japan was oval and elongated, and the silver wire dengi of the Russian principalities in the fourteenth and fifteenth centuries produced some of the oddest and most eccentric shapes. From these developed the kopeks of 1534–1718, which were cut from heavy silver wire and then hammered into ovals.

Below: Klippe of Ulm, Germany: a circular design struck on a diamond-shaped blank.

Many medieval coins are scyphate, or cup-shaped. These curious concave coins originated in the Byzantine Empire in the tenth century but the fashion spread throughout the Balkans and Cyprus. The best-known examples are the gold nomisma, but scyphates were also minted in copper, silver and electrum. Prince Frederick-Henry of Orange (1625–47) struck scyphate coins that were uniface and concave. These *schusselheller* were in denominations of deniers and obols and were struck in billon or copper.

Square Coins

Square coins range from the copper Indo-Scythian examples of pre-Christian times to the Afghan aspers of the nineteenth century. Many German and Scandinavian states in the late medieval period struck coins in a square or lozenge format, known as klippe or klipping. In some cases the dies for circular coins were merely struck on square flans, but in other instances special dies were employed, with ornaments occupying the spandrels (the spaces between the arc of the circle and the corners of the square). The Moghul emperor Jahangir (1605–27) issued round and square rupees in alternate months. Modern square coins include the 5c of Sri Lanka (Ceylon) from 1909 to 1971, the Dutch 5c of 1941, the Burmese 10p since 1952, the Philippines 1c since 1975 and the Bangladesh 5p of 1973–80, and Poland struck klippe in

Above left: a large diamond-shaped 10 shilling coin, issued by Jersey to celebrate the ninth centenary of the Norman Conquest, 1966; above right: Japan: *Isshu Gin* (one shu silver), mid nineteenth century; lower right: Ceylon: obverse of the square five cents, 1971.

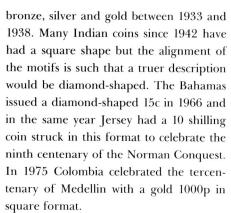

Triangular Coins

Several countries have issued triangular coins. The first coinage of Gabon (1883) included a 10 centime with three truncated sides and a triangular 20 centime, both being cut from sheet zinc. In 1988, the Cook Islands introduced a series that included a three-sided $2 coin. This coin, like the vast majority of four-sided coins, has rounded corners to avoid sharp edges. The disadvantages of triangular and square coins, even with rounded edges, is that they do not roll, which means that they are unsuitable in slot machines and coin-operated vending equipment. For this purpose, only circular and polygonal coins with seven or more sides are practical.

Above: Diamond-shaped pound coins of Jersey (1981) and India, square coins from Sri Lanka and Malaya and a triangular coin from the Cook Islands.

bronze, silver and gold between 1933 and 1938. Many Indian coins since 1942 have had a square shape but the alignment of the motifs is such that a truer description would be diamond-shaped. The Bahamas issued a diamond-shaped 15c in 1966 and in the same year Jersey had a 10 shilling coin struck in this format to celebrate the ninth centenary of the Norman Conquest. In 1975 Colombia celebrated the tercentenary of Medellin with a gold 1000p in square format.

Many-sided Coins

Polygonal coins may be found in many parts of the world. Belize had a $100 coin in 1981 with five sides. Six-sided coins have included Djibouti's 50c of 1921–2, Egypt's 2p of 1944 and the commemorative $100 coins from the British Virgin Islands (1982–3). The UK pioneered heptagonal coins in 1969, when the 50 new pence coin was introduced as a prelude to decimal currency. This format was subsequently adopted by countries as far afield as

Left: Heptagonal (seven-sided) coins from UK, Mexico, Tonga and the Isle of Man.

Left: Dodecagonal (twelve-sided) coins from the Cook Islands, Australia and the Seychelles.

Gibraltar, the Falkland Islands, Barbados and Tonga. Augsburg issued eight-sided heller in 1744–76, while 10-sided coins have been issued by Afghanistan (1979), Colombia (1967) and the Dominican Republic (1983). Dodecagons or 12-sided coins range from the British brass three-pence of 1937–67 to Australia's 50c since 1969 and Botswana's 2 thebe of 1981. Argentina favoured this format for various denominations from 1964 to 1978 and they may also be found from Chile, Colombia, Cyprus and Fiji in recent years.

Wavy-edged Coins

Numerous coins have been issued with a scalloped or wavy edge. This device has found favour with many African and Oriental countries where a largely illiterate population can recognize the value of the different coins by their shape. The Moghul Empire probably holds the record for the most shapes used by a single country, with round, square, diamond, elliptical, triangular and rectangular (oblong) coins, and this tradition has been maintained to some extent by modern India and Sri Lanka. While Jersey had a 12-sided threepenny, like the UK, neighbouring Guernsey preferred a coin with a scalloped edge. Variations in the sides of coins may also be adopted in cases where new values are added to the series and a different shape is preferable to merely increasing the size. Thus the UK avoided the need for a coin

of five times the size and weight of the 10p coin by issuing the heptagonal 50p. Hong Kong was forced to face the dilemma of already having quite a large dollar coin when it was decided, in 1975, to introduce a $2 piece. The problem was neatly solved by using a coin of much the same weight, but having a scalloped edge. A $5 coin, only slightly larger, was issued in 1976–9, with 10 sides.

Coins with Holes

Apart from the shape, the appearance of a coin can be determined by the presence of a hole in the middle. Chinese *cash* and other cast coins of the Far East were produced with a square hole in the centre so that large amounts could be strung together for the sake of convenience. Usually they were strung together as if they were stacked, but sometimes you will come across *cash* which

Below: Scalloped coins from Israel, Hong Kong and Sri Lanka (top row), the Cook Islands and Hong Kong (bottom row). The middle coin of the lower row is a curiosity – a British 10p struck in a Hong Kong scalloped collar. Thousands were shipped out to Hong Kong and issued as $2 coins before the error was detected.

Above: Holed coins (top row): Denmark, Japan and Hungary; (bottom row) all Laos, showing the piercing of pictorial motifs.

have been cleverly strung in an overlapping pattern to form 'swords' or long rods. In the Western world, where coins were usually struck rather than cast, the provision of a central hole did not emerge until 1863, when Heaton of Birmingham struck 1 mil coins for Hong Kong with a central hole, emulating the *cash* previously used. In 1887 Paris struck bronze sapeques for French Indo-China with a square central hole. Bronze cents were at first struck in the conventional form but from 1896 they had a circular central hole and this practice eventually extended to denominations from the quarter cent to the 5 cents. British West Africa's base metal coins from 1907 onwards also had holes and this set the trend for many other colonial issues, thus enabling primitive peoples (without purses or pockets) to string their money together.

Many European coins since the 1920s have also been holed, but for a different reason. Where it is laid down by law that a certain denomination must be of a particu-

lar weight, one way of extending the surface area is to insert a hole and thereby increase the diameter. Norway adopted this expedient in 1921 to avoid reducing the size of coins whose weight had to comply with the regulations of the Scandinavian Monetary Union. Denmark followed suit in 1924 with a view to enlarging the overall size of its coins.

Putting a hole through a coin, however, limits the design possibilities. Making a virtue of necessity, French Indo-China and British West Africa made the holes the focal points of geometric designs, while the holed coins of Scandinavia and France have rearranged the elements of the design, such as the date, denomination, heraldry and inscriptions, around the hole.

Albania's 50 leke coin of 1988, commemorating the country's railway system, has an off-centre hole simulating a railway tunnel out of which emerges a steam loco on one side and a modern diesel electric on the other!

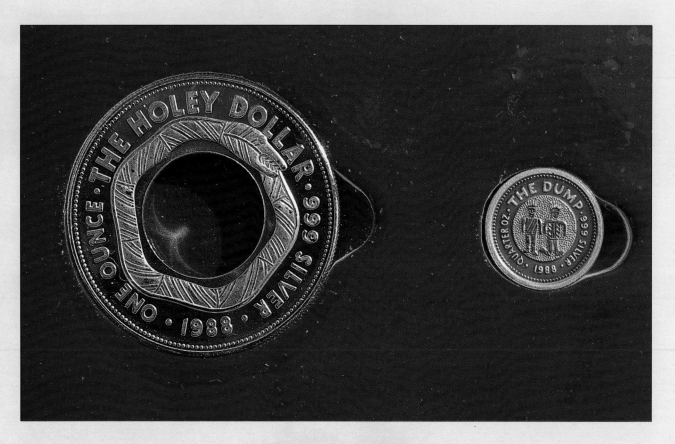

**THE DUMP AND THE
HOLEY DOLLAR**

Holed coins do not, as a rule, permit a portrait or pictorial motifs, but Australia managed to achieve both in a very curious coin of 1988. This was, in fact, one of a pair of coins that celebrated the 175th anniversary of Australia's first distinctive coins. In 1813 Lachlan Macquarie, Governor of New South Wales, having procured 40,000 Spanish dollars at 4s 9d each,

had their centres cut out. The centres, known as 'dumps', were counter-marked FIFTEEN PENCE *and put into circulation, while the outer rings, which came to be known as 'holey dollars', were countermarked with the name of the colony, the date and a new value of five shillings. The canny governor thus made a profit of 1s 6d on each Spanish dollar.*

In the 1988 silver coins, the holey dollar had a face value of $1, whereas the corresponding dump was valued at 25c. The dump bore the profile of Queen Elizabeth on the obverse and Aboriginal figures on the reverse, but a tiny version of the Queen's profile appeared at the top of the holey dollar, while the reverse had an Aboriginal snake pattern draped around the hole.

THICKNESS

Because the earliest coins were struck from lumps of metal, they tended to be fairly thick with rounded edges and high relief. In Roman times, however, coins generally became much thinner and during the Middle Ages they were thinner still. The silver pennies of medieval England have a rather tinny appearance. Even the gold coins minted in Europe up to the seven- teenth century seem surprisingly thin. The technique of cutting blanks with shears out of hammered plates of metal tended to encourage this fashion, for thin plates were obviously much easier to cut to the required shape than thick plates. By the same token, however, the thinness of coins made it that much easier for dishonest persons to clip off some of the precious metal from the edge.

Bracteates

In the twelfth century the mints of Thuringia (southeast Germany) began striking very thin coins, known in their own time as *Hohlpfennige* (literally 'hollow pennies'). Only one die was used as the flan was so thin that the impression showed through on the other side in reverse.

Known as bracteates, these spread throughout the Germanic world, from Switzerland to Poland, and flourished for about 200 years. They often circulated alongside coins of more orthodox thickness and appearance and it is thought that they were intended for restricted circulation of some special purpose (such as the payment of taxes). An alternative theory suggests that they were devised as a method of making the coins appear as large as before, despite a reduction in their actual weight. Bracteates, however, varied considerably in size and appearance, from quite small coins with a very high relief, like die-stamped metal buttons, to coins with a very large diameter and quite shallow relief. Some of them are literally paper thin and have to be handled with the utmost care to avoid causing damage.

Silver Coins

When the Swiss canton of Berne introduced a silver coin worth a third of a florin in 1492, it was soon named a dicken (from the German word for thick). It was very much thicker than the testoons of Italy, which were then very popular and which had set the standard for the larger silver coins of many countries about that time. The greater abundance of silver in the sixteenth century encouraged heavier and thicker coins, and the development of rolling machinery and

the screw press also made such coins easier to produce. A flan of even thickness was a characteristic of the beautiful milled coins produced by Mestrell and Briot and set them apart from the usual hammered coins of the period.

Practical Limitations

For most practical purposes, there are limits to how thick a coin can be. The thickest British coins in general circulation were the copper twopence of 1797, nicknamed 'Cartwheels' on account of their massive size and raised rims. At that time it was decreed that coins had to have an intrinsic value equal to their face value. Thus the twopenny coins had to contain copper of that value, and as copper was then worth a penny an ounce it followed that the coins had to weigh 2 oz (56.7 g) each. They had a diameter of 41 mm (anything larger would have been awkward for pockets and purses) and the thickness was the only other variation possible. Not surprisingly, they were not minted after the initial year of issue. When the first base-metal pound coins were issued (by the Isle of Man) in 1978, they were struck in a magnetized cupro-nickel-zinc compound known as virenium, but the diameter and thickness were based on the gold sovereign. As gold has a higher specific gravity than virenium, this meant that the new coins were a lot lighter. In 1981, Guernsey followed suit with a cupro-nickel-zinc coin of the same diameter, but it was made more substantial by virtually doubling the weight (and hence the thickness) and this option was chosen by the Royal Mint for the UK pound coins introduced in 1983. The Isle of Man then came into line with the UK by increasing the weight and thickness of its pound coins accordingly.

PRESENTATION PIECES

On 28 December 1335, the King of France signed a decree authorizing the issue of piéforts. These were coins struck from normal dies but using flans two or three times the usual thicknesses and weight. The very thick edge of these coins was often ornamentally engraved or inscribed, testifying to their use as presentation pieces. When Henry VII of England introduced the gold sovereign in 1489, he had some pieces of twice or three times the normal thickness struck for presentation to courtiers and foreign dignitaries. About 1570, King Philip II of Spain struck double and treble coins, a practice continued by Albert and Isabella in the Netherlands, hence the double albertins, double patagons and other very thick coins of the late sixteenth century. It was in France, however, that piéforts attained their greatest popularity. Eventually they were struck on a regular basis for sale to collectors, and this practice continues to the present day. The idea was taken up by the Royal Mint in 1982 and since then many coins have been struck on flans of double the normal thickness. These modern piéforts are usually struck in a different metal from the normal coins. For example, the British pound coins are minted in a cupro-nickel alloy, whereas the piéforts are produced in sterling silver.

SIZE

The size of coins has varied enormously over the centuries, both between coins of different value, as one might expect, and also between coins of the same face value.

'Shrinking' Coinage

An excellent example of this was provided in June 1990 when Great Britain reduced the size of its 5p coins, from 23.595 mm to 18 mm, while retaining the design and alloy. This was quite a shock because the 5p, and its pre-decimal equivalent, the shilling, had remained constant since 1816. However, even the shilling of 1816 was considerably smaller than its ancestor, the testoon of Henry VII, which was introduced about 1504 and had a diameter of 30 mm.

Other countries could produce far more dramatic examples of shrinking coinage. The Mexican peso had a diameter of 39 mm and contained .786 troy ounce of silver until 1914 when minting was temporarily suspended during the First World War. When minting was resumed in 1918 it had shrunk to 33 mm and the fineness was similarly reduced, so that the actual silver content was only .4663 troy ounce. The diameter remained constant until 1967 although the silver was progressively debased until latterly the coin contained only .0514 troy ounce. After another gap, it re-emerged in 1970 as a cupro-nickel coin with a diameter of 29.5 mm and continued until 1983. By that time its real value had sunk to half a US cent! Since then it has plummeted to less than a 10th of that value and even the 100 peso coin (currently the smallest in circulation) is virtually worthless.

Above: Mexico: pesos of 1963, 1978 and 1984 in descending order of size.

Left: UK: 5 new pence (1971) and 5 pence (1990), showing the reduction in size.

Smallest . . .

In 1904 Panama introduced a 2½ centesimo coin of 9 mm, weighing a mere 1.25 g. Popularly known as a 'Panama pill' or 'Panama pearl', it was reintroduced in 1975 and since then has been struck by the Royal Canadian Mint or the Franklin Mint of Philadelphia. More recently, the People's Republic of China issued a $10 gold coin honouring Marco Polo. This has a diameter of 9 mm and contains .0347 troy ounce of pure gold. These are veritable giants compared with some of the really tiny coins from other parts of the world. In 1328, the Ottoman Empire introduced the akce, which contained 1.2 g of pure silver and had a diameter of 7 mm. For really tiny coins, however, we have to go right back to classical times. The obol or sixth drachma had a diameter of 10 mm, but Cumae had a quarter obol of 3 mm and Neapolis a coin of the same value with a diameter of only 2.5 mm. Cumae had a sixth obol (diameter 2 mm) but Athens capped that with the hemitetartemorion or eighth obol. It seems odd that one of the longest names should be bestowed on one of the smallest coins. Barely 2 mm in diameter and correspondingly thin, this coin must have posed a problem to Athenian shoppers. They devised a cunning method of carrying such small change – they put them in their mouths. In *Wasps*, Aristophanes has one of his characters say:

> For once
> Lysistratus, the funny fool, played me
> the scurviest trick. We'd got a drachma
> between us; he changed it at the fish
> stall, then laid me down three mullet
> scales. I thought them obols and popped
> them in my mouth. Oh, the vile smell.
> Ugh! I spat them out and collared him!

Incidentally the hemitetartemorion was the price of a glass of wine in ancient Athens. Inflation hit the Roman Empire in the fourth and fifth centuries AD and the silver denarius gave way to the billon or copper minim (from the Latin *minimus*, smallest). These averaged 2–3 mm in diameter, but some *minimissimi*, from the Lydney Park hoard discovered in 1929, were little bigger than a pinhead.

Left: Colombia: gold peso – one of the tiny gold coins current in the nineteenth century and especially popular in Latin America.

THE FARTHING

In bygone times, when coins possessed an intrinsic value equivalent or close to their face value, the size of coins reflected the everyday needs of the people. In Tudor times even a farthing (a quarter of a penny) had real spending power. Because England (unlike many other European countries) took a pride in issuing even the humblest coins in a high silver standard, the usual practice was to cut a silver penny into four, made easier because of the cross on the reverse. Farthings as separate coins were struck from the time of Edward I onwards, but by the reign of Queen Elizabeth I the value of the farthing had dwindled to the point at which it was more trouble to mint than it was worth. Because a farthing was still needed in small change, however, the Mint devised an ingenious solution to the problem. Silver pennies and halfpence continued to be struck as before, but a three-farthing coin was added to the series. Because these coins did not bear their actual denomination, it was necessary to distinguish between the new coin and the existing denominations. This was achieved by adding a rose to the obverse, behind the queen's head. This was alluded to by Shakespeare in King John:

> *. . . my face so thin*
> *That in mine ear I durst not stick*
>   *a rose*
> *Lest men should say, 'Look, where*
> *threefarthings goes!'*

The silver farthing, last minted in the reign of King Edward VI, about 1551, had a diameter of only 9 mm, making it the smallest English coin.

Largest . . .

I have already mentioned the cumbersome Cartwheel twopence of 1797, but there have been even larger coins. The Roman coins known as *aes grave* (heavy bronze) included such monsters as the dupondius, quincussis and decussis weighing two, five and ten Roman pounds, respectively. The last named weighed a massive 2,730 g. The Chinese province of Fukien had cast copper or zinc 100 *cash* coins in the name of the Emperor Hsien Feng in the 1850s with diameters ranging from 70–78 mm. Even larger coins of 500 and 1,000 cash have been reported from Fukien but none has been positively confirmed and it is possible that they may have been fantasy pieces. Fantasy pieces are coins perpetrated for collects, without any legality or government authority.

These heavy base-metal coins reflected the cheapness of copper compared to silver or gold, but some really large coins have been struck in precious metals too. Duke Julius of Brunswick (1568–89) hit upon a novel method of making his subjects save money. Each citizen was obliged to hold a certain number of coins known as Julius-löser, according to the amount of their property and income, to be redeemed only in times of emergency. Thus these coins formed a reserve of public treasure. The coins were struck in silver, in denominations up to 16 thalers, and Duke Julius reserved the right to exchange them at a later date in smaller coins of a lesser fineness. When the duke died, in 1589, his duchy was very prosperous; the state was free of debt and the treasury was able to boast a surplus of 700,000 thalers.

The largest English gold coin was a sovereign piéfort of King Henry VII struck on a blank of treble weight and thickness. This contained over 45 g of gold but had a diameter of only 41 mm. The largest English gold coin ever struck was the triple unite struck at Shrewsbury and Oxford during the Civil War. These handsome coins measured 45 mm and were tariffed at 60 shillings, but their weight was only 28 g. By contrast, the five-guinea pieces of Charles II had a diameter of 39 mm and a weight of 42.7 g, while the five-pound coins of the present day have a diameter of 36 mm and

Right: The raw material of modern gold coins: granular gold extracted from crushed ore looks like dried cake and crumbles readily.

Left: Refining and smelting gold at the Royal Canadian Mint, Ottawa.

Left: The molten gold is poured into fire-resistant moulds and cast into ingots prior to rolling into coinage strip.

a weight of 39.8 g with an actual gold content of 1.1771 troy ounces. The largest US gold coin was the $50 of 1915, commemorating the Panama-Pacific Exposition; this weighed in at 83.59 g and had a diameter of 41 mm.

The Venetian Republic went in for some outsize gold coins in the eighteenth century. The 24 zecchini (sequins) of the Doges Paolo Renier (1779–89) and Lodovico Manin (1789–97) contained 83.68 g of almost pure gold, with a diameter of 50 mm. Paolo Renier struck even larger coins, of 30, 40, 50 and 55 zecchini, the last named with a weight of 192 g and a diameter of 76 mm. Under Alviso Moecenigo (1763–78) 60 and 100 zecchini were struck, but Lodovico Manin had the last word; his stupendous 105 zecchini weighed in at 367.41 g of .999 gold and had a diameter of 79 mm. Sigismond III of Poland struck 100 ducat coins in 1621, containing 12.5 troy ounces, and similar coins were minted by Michael Apafi in neighbouring Transylvania (1674–7). Spain also favoured ultra-large gold coins in the late fifteenth century. John II of Castile struck an enormous coin known

as the Cavalier d'or, or 20 dobla, which weighed 90 g and had a diameter of 93 mm. In very recent years there has been a rash of very large and heavy gold coins. In the 1980s the People's Republic of China issued the 1,000 yuan panda coin containing 12 troy ounces, but this was soon surpassed by Gibraltar (15 oz) and the Isle of Man (25 oz). These enormous coins, however, were easily beaten by the gold multiple mohurs of the Moghul Empire. The Emperor Jahangir issued 100 mohurs in 1639 with a diameter of 97 mm and a weight of 2,094 g. The British Museum has a plaster cast of a 200 mohur that was later melted down, while 500 mohur coins were mentioned in Jahangir's autobiography. The French traveller Jean-Baptiste Tavernier mentioned even larger coins, which he had seen in Jahangir's treasury, but they were all thought to have been melted down until a magnificent specimen of 1,000 mohurs turned up in 1987. It weighed 12 kg and has a diameter of 203 mm. This fantastic coin, minted at Agra in 1613, was offered for auction in Geneva but failed to reach its reserve price of $10 million.

RIMS AND EDGES

These terms may seem synonymous but collectors distinguish between them. The rim is that part of the surface of a coin at its circumference. It plays an important role in modern coins for it both protects the surfaces of the coin and helps in stacking. This was not a matter that concerned the minters of hammered coins and it is virtually impossible to stack these one on top of the other without them falling over.

The rim is a line of raised metal running round the perimeter. Rims may be thick or thin, plain or beaded. A good example of a coin with very thick rims would be the Cartwheel twopence. In this case the rims are said to be raised, and because they extended inwards for 4 mm, the legends were inscribed on them in incuse lettering. This unusual style was revived in 1985 for the British seven-sided 20p coin and it has since been employed most effectively in several Manx coins that have the obverse rim indented to allow for the pointed truncation of the Queen's bust.

In the vast majority of modern coins, however, the rim is relatively thin. Within the rim there is usually a ring of fine ornaments, either circular beads or elongated teeth. This is the kind of detail that tends to vary from one die to another and collectors looking for minute variations are often reduced to counting these beads. One British coin that has no beading is the 50 pence piece; the obsolete 12-sided threepence

Top: Isle of Man: silver crown showing an incuse inscription on a raised rim, 1987.

Middle: UK: Cartwheel twopence, 1797, with a portrait of King George III on the obverse and an incuse inscription round the raised rim.

Bottom: Circular coins with polygonal frames: USA (Anthony dollar, 1979), India (rupee, 1985) and France (2 francs, 1979).

was another. On the other hand, beading is absent from the current series of US coins, although it was a feature of all of the preceding issues. The cupro-nickel dollar of 1979, portraying the suffragist Susan B. Anthony, was unusual in having a 13-sided rim on both sides, within a circular format.

The side of the coin viewed end on is described as the edge. In hammered coins the edge was usually left plain, although a notable exception comprises Roman coins of the first and second centuries BC. These appear to have nicked edges, but the nicks were quite regular and were a deliberate part of the coin production. Just why these coins were serrated remains a mystery. One school of thought maintains that they were thus indented to show the purity of the metal, but as most of the serrated coins were of base metal that was silver-plated, the serration must have served some other purpose. It has been argued that these coins were intended for circulation among the Celtic tribes, who had a penchant for serrated ring amulets.

Milling and Graining

The experimental milled coins of Eloi Mestrell and Nicholas Briot had plain edges but great attention was paid to the regularity of the flans and the beaded rims. The beading of the rims would have deterred people from clipping off slivers of precious metal to the same extent that these were clipped from the hammered coins. In 1662, however, when milled coins were adopted in England on a permanent basis, added security was provided by adorning the edges with a pattern of fine grooves, running across the edge at right angles to the rim. The layman often refers to this as 'milling' but this is a misnomer. The numismatic term for this is graining. The grain on British and US coins usually consists of these fine vertical serrations. In some cases, coins have been recorded with a fine or coarse grain, and counting the notches provides the variety searchers with yet another method of going cross-eyed. An interrupted grain may be found on the 50c coins of New Zealand and the pound coins of the Isle of Man, its main purpose being to assist blind or partially sighted people to distinguish between coins of high and low value. In some countries the graining takes the form of short lines set at an angle, and this is known as a cable edge. Still others prefer an edge in which close beading is contained in a sandwich of thicker horizontal lines. This type of edge is to be found on the current Hong Kong $5 coins. Many European and Latin American countries have used a decorative edge consisting of floral or geometric ornaments, either standing out in relief or cut into the edge (incuse).

Inscriptions

Another very popular form of edge decoration consists of inscriptions. This appeared on the larger coins of Charles II, when milling was adopted in 1662. These coins bore the Latin inscription DECUS ET TUTAMEN ANNO REGNI followed by a numeral (an ornament and a safeguard in the . . . year of the reign). This alluded to the fact that the inscription was not only ornamental but deterred people from clipping the edge. When the British pound coin was introduced in 1983, the Royal Mint revived this motto, inscribing it incuse in addition to vertical graining. Usually edges have either graining or an inscription, but seldom both together, although you will find this on certain Canadian £100 gold coins which bear the country name across the graining.

Below: Unconventional edges: 'sandwich' (Hong Kong $5) and 'interrupted graining' (New Zealand 50c).

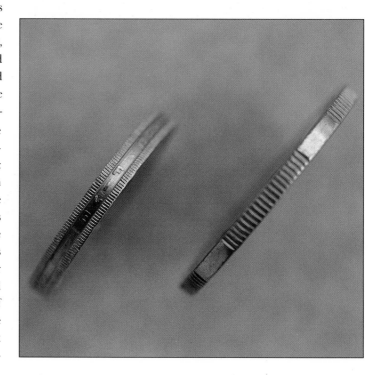

HOW COINS ARE INSCRIBED

Edge ornament and inscriptions are usually added to coins after the obverse and reverse have been struck, using a rocking bar with the ornament on a strip of steel resembling a spring. Alternatively, the collar that surrounds the blank can be engraved with the desired ornament. When the coin is struck, the immense pressure causes the metal to flow and fill the grooves and recesses of the dies. The metal will also fill any spaces that are within the collar.

Inscriptions on coin edges vary enormously. In 1951 the UK struck a crown to celebrate the Festival of Britain, which, in turn, commemorated the centenary of the Great Exhibition. The coin itself did not differ in design from its predecessors, but the commemorative element was built into the edge, which was inscribed in Latin: CIVIUM INDUSTRIA FLORET CIVITAS (by the industry of its citizens the state flourishes). Two years later, however, the Coronation crown had an incuse inscription in English: FAITH AND TRUTH I WILL BEAR UNTO YOU.

As a rule, edge graining and inscriptions are confined to circular coins. Coins with a scalloped or polygonal edge are usually plain-edged, but a notable exception was provided by the Isle of Man, which issued a 50p coin in 1979 for the Manx Millennium Viking Voyage. Subsequently, these coins were reissued with an incuse inscription round the edge H.M. / Q.E. II / ROYAL / VISIT / I.O.M. / JULY / 1979, each portion occupying one of the seven sides. As the inscription was applied after the coins had been struck it was impossible to ensure that the inscription began at the same point on each coin or that the coins were obverse-up or -down at the time of striking. As a consequence, the inscription may be found upright or inverted relative to the obverse and in any one of the seven sides, so that 14 collectable varieties resulted.

Below: Isle of Man: 50p Millennium of Tynwald, 5 July 1979 – a rare instance of a coin bearing the day and month as well as the year of issue.

The Parts of a Coin

Many collectors concentrate on coins of certain sizes or metals, but the vast majority collect them either according to the country of issue or the subjects depicted on them. Still others make a study of the epigraphy (the inscriptions found on coins) and even the cryptic marks and symbols.

PORTRAITURE

The Ancient World

The obverse, the lower die, is subject to less wear than the reverse, or upper die, and so tends to have the more important device on it. In ancient Greece the portrait of a god or goddess was usually featured on the obverse. This practice was followed by Philip II and Alexander the Great, with Zeus on the obverse and his attribute, an eagle, on the reverse. After his death, Alexander himself was regarded as a god and for this reason his portrait began to appear on the coins of the Hellenistic kingdoms into which his empire was divided. In these portraits Alexander was shown with the horns of Ammon sprouting from his temples as a sign of his divinity.

Gradually the idea of portraying a ruler in his or her lifetime became acceptable. The coins of the Seleucid empire and Egypt provide many fine examples. We find, for example, that Cleopatra was not as beautiful as her reputation suggests – if the beaky profile on her coins is anything to go by!

Roman Coins

The Roman Republic preferred figures from mythology and female allegories of abstract ideas such as Concord, Abundance and Victory. Significantly, Julius Caesar, who had ambitions to become the greatest Roman of them all, was the first to be depicted on coins during his lifetime, in 44 BC. After Caesar was assassinated, Brutus issued silver denarii with his own portrait on the obverse. This coin also provides an interesting early attempt to use coins as a propaganda medium, for the reverse shows the cap of Liberty between two daggers, with the inscription EID MAR, a none too subtle reference to the murder of Caesar in the name of liberty, on the Ides of March.

Lysimachus, who succeeded to much of the empire of Alexander the Great, struck silver tetradrachms at Alexandria and Pergamon with the head of Alexander the Great (obverse – above) and the seated figure of Athena with a shield and spear (reverse – below). The latter motif was plagiarized for the Britannia design on British pennies more than 2,000 years later.

Thereafter Roman coins were outstanding for the realism of their portraiture. Usually the emperor was shown in profile (side-face) and very rarely was a facing portrait used, although there were some notable exceptions on the coins of Postumus, Licinius I and Licinius II. Not only the emperor, but his empress and even the princes and princesses of the royal line were shown on coins. There was a fascinating series of family coins under Septimius Severus, which depicted his wife, Julia Domna, his daughter-in-law, Plautilla, and his two sons, Caracalla and Geta, as well as himself. On an aureus of AD 201, for example, Septimius Severus appeared alone on the obverse, while the reverse bore a facing bust of Julia Domna between confronting busts of her two sons. Caligula issued a sestertius that had, on the reverse, portraits of his three sisters, Agrippina, Drusilla and Julia.

When the Roman Empire in the West collapsed in the late fifth century, the art of coinage disappeared. The empire continued in the East, with its headquarters at Byzantium (Constantinople), and the style of portraiture continued. The Byzantine Empire, however, developed some peculiarities in this regard; many coins showed facing portraits of Jesus Christ, sometimes flanked by apostles or saints, and full-length portraits of rulers, either seated or standing, came into vogue. Portraits became more stereotyped and less realistic than during the heyday of the Roman Empire.

The Dark Ages

During the Dark Ages the coins of Europe degenerated. The barbarian tribes who overran the empire struck coins on Roman models, but they lacked the skills, techniques and equipment to produce the same results. The petty rulers of the Anglo-Saxon kingdoms might portray themselves with the laurels and togas of their Roman predecessors, but the results were crude in the extreme. The technique of engraving dies by means of 'dot and squiggle' punches did nothing for the art of portraiture either, and some of the portraits on coins of Kent and Wessex in the early ninth century are

Below: One of the most prolific and beautiful series was that issued by the Popes as the temporal rulers of the Papal States. The coins were well designed and were among the first in the world to be struck on the screw press invented by Donato Bramante. The coins are rich in colourful religious symbolism. The arms on the scudo depicted the papal tiara or triple crown above the crossed keys of St Peter. The reverse motifs (right) were inspired by biblical subjects, but also showed the influence of the Baroque as in this coin of 1694 showing the female allegory of Plenty with a cornucopia. The Latin motto EGENO ET PAVPERI signifies 'for the needy and the poor'.

well beyond the point of caricature. In this period, facing portraits were seldom used, although notable exceptions were the unique gold solidus of York, showing a facing bust of Archbishop Wigmund (837–54) and the silver pennies of Canterbury, showing Archbishop Ceolnoth (833–70). Edward the Confessor (1042–66) revived this concept towards the end of his reign and a high proportion of the pennies of William the Conqueror adopted the same style. Out of this developed a conventional full-face portrait of the king. You could tell that it was the king because there was some semblance of a crown on his head and often a sceptre sticking up awkwardly in the corner. Eyes, nose and mouth were indicated by appropriate dots and lines applied by punches, and a few pellets or squiggles at the side served to suggest locks of hair. In this manner developed the immobilized portrait that graced English coins until the time of Henry VII. To be sure, there were vast improvements in the engraving of dies as the centuries progressed, but the king was invariably shown as a fresh-faced, smiling youth with flowing locks, whether or not he was, in reality, bearded or clean-shaven, bald or with one foot in the grave. At the beginning of the sixteenth century, however, Henry VII abandoned such immobilized portraits, and the profile issue, engraved by Alexander Brugsal, showed an English monarch for the first time as he really looked.

The Rise of Realism

England differed in no respect from other European countries in the Middle Ages; everywhere immobilized portraits were the norm. In 1463, however, the Italian city-state of Milan began issuing coins showing Duke Francesco I Sforza as he really was. Under his successor, Galeazzo-Maria Sforza, Milan adopted a silver lira, originally nicknamed a grossone on account of its large size but later better known as a testone (from the Italian word *testa*, a head). With the advent of this beautiful coin in 1474, modern coinage may be said to have begun. Milan even had coins with dual portraits; in 1481 testoni were issued with the portrait of Gian-Galeazzo on one side and his uncle, the regent Ludovico, on the reverse.

Louis XII of France struck portrait coins in 1500–12 in his capacity as Duke of Milan, and brought the idea back to France where the name was spelled *teston*. From France realistic portraits spread to England, the large coin worth 12 pence being known initially as a testoon. Portrait coinage spread rapidly throughout Europe, the last immobilized portrait coins being the silver 5 sueldos of Majorca and Valentia in 1556, modelled on English groats of the fifteenth century. Since then portraits have become more and more realistic, even if the result was hardly flattering. Arguably the ugliest portrait is that found on Austrian thalers of 1682 showing the Archduke Leopold I whose Habsburg jaw (a family characteristic) was exceptionally exaggerated.

People must have thought that Britain had returned to the era of the immobilized portrait during the reign of Queen Victoria. As late as 1887, many of her coins depicted her as a teenager, although by that time she had reigned for half a century and was 68 years old.

Full Face versus Profile?

For practical purposes, a profile is preferable to a full-face portrait. A profile relies mainly on the distinctive outline of the effigy for realism and other features can be suggested by means of a few subtle lines without materially affecting the height of the relief. In modern coins, where the ability to stack neatly is a decided advantage, low relief is essential and this can only be achieved satisfactorily by means of a profile. In some modern coins, such as the current Dutch series, this has been reduced to the two-dimensional character of a silhouette. A facing bust, on the other hand, generally requires a fairly high relief to show the distinctive features. Unfortunately, noses tend to stick out prominently and this upsets the balance of the design. The even more unfortunate results from combining a full-face portrait with debased silver in the coinage of Henry VIII have already been discussed (see page 00). After the wretched 'Coppernoses' it is hardly surprising that facing busts were never again used in Britain, but this does not mean that full-face portraits have not been used in modern times. The Cayman Islands and the Isle of Man have had full-face coins on several occasions in

Above: Facing portraits: Isle of Man (Sir Winston Churchill), Senegal (Leopold Senghor), Thailand (Kings Vijiravudh and Phumibol), Korea (Admiral Lee Sun-shin) and Mexico (Guadelupe Victoria).

Below: Isle of Man crown (1987) commemorating the bicentenary of the American Constitution. It shows the Statue of Liberty and portraits of statesmen, from George Washington to Ronald Reagan.

recent years. Both issued coins in 1974, with facing portaits of Winston Churchill to celebrate the centenary of his birth. In 1977 the Cayman Islands marked the Silver Jubilee of Queen Elizabeth by issuing a set of five dollar-sized coins, portraying the queens regnant from Mary I to Victoria. An even more ambitious series of 1980 featured the monarchs of England from Edward the Confessor to the present day and used facing busts in the majority of instances. Side-by-side facing portraits of Prince Charles and Lady Diana Spencer appeared on gold coins of 1981 celebrating the royal wedding. The Isle of Man has had some very striking silver crowns portraying Prince Philip and the disabled air ace Sir Douglas Bader, while a crown of 1987 bore a stunning array of American presidential portraits, from George Washington to Ronald Reagan. The late Emperor Hirohito of Japan appeared full-face on coins of Liberia, while many of the crowns of recent years, in honour of Queen Elizabeth the Queen Mother, have portrayed her full-face.

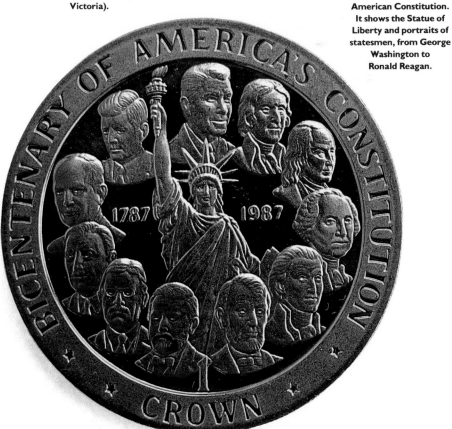

Coins of Their Time

Sometimes the portraits on coins are at odds with the prevailing political situation. Philip II of Spain was portrayed on coins of the Netherlands up to 1581, although this region of his realm had been in revolt since 1577. Charles I continued to appear on English coins despite the fact that the Tower Mint was controlled by Parliament during the Civil War. In France, Louis XIV continued to appear on coins after the revolution broke out in 1789, although there was a subtle change in his title. Previously his name and titles had been rendered in Latin and included a reference to the grace of God, but in 1792–3 Louis was styled as 'King of the French' (rather than of France), in French, and without any mention of God's grace. Only after he lost his head to the guillotine was his effigy dropped.

Below: USA: circulating coinage portraying Abraham Lincoln (1c), Thomas Jefferson (5c), Franklin D. Roosevelt (10c), John F. Kennedy (50c) and Dwight Eisenhower ($1).

DEAD HEADS

Kings and queens, emperors and empresses, princes, dukes and presidents have graced the coins of many countries, but the US has a rule that no living person should be portrayed on a coin; George Washington himself resolutely rejected such a suggestion when he became the first president in 1789, on the grounds that it smacked of monarchy and was out of place in a republic. However, this has not prevented the use of portraits of people after their death. As far as the general circulating coinage is concerned, this convention began with the cent in 1909 when a bust of Abraham Lincoln replaced the head of an Indian chief. This was intended as a mark of respect at the time of Lincoln's birth centenary, but he has remained ever since. In 1932, Washington was placed on the quarter dollar, followed by Thomas Jefferson on the nickel (1938) and Benjamin Franklin on the half dollar (1948). Franklin Delano Roosevelt died in 1945 and as a tribute to him his portrait was placed on the dimes from 1946 onwards. Similarly, John F. Kennedy appeared on the half dollar in 1964, shortly after his assassination – notwithstanding a federal law that stated that the design of a coin must remain unchanged for at least a quarter of a century (the Franklin design had only been in use for 17 years). When the minting of silver dollars was resumed in 1971, Dwight D. Eisenhower was chosen for the obverse.

After the execution of King Louis, France replaced his portrait with various allegorical motifs, inspired by classical art. The bust of a female wearing the Phrygian cap of liberty graced the obverse of the bronze and silver coins, while a winged figure, symbolizing the law, appeared on the gold pieces. It was the French example that the US followed when its first coins were introduced in 1794, bearing the head of Liberty.

Muslim Law

The earliest Islamic coins were closely modelled on their Byzantine or Sassanian contemporaries; but in AD 76 the Khalif Abd al-Malik banned the use of portraits, in compliance with a rule of the Prophet Muhammad, who prohibited the making of representations of living things. This ban on the depiction of living persons has continued to the present time, although it was ignored by the Emperor Jahangir, who contrived to break the Muslim ban on alcohol as well; his mohurs of 1611–14 showed him holding a cup of wine! From the beginning of this century the Shahs of Persia ignored the Islamic ban and placed their effigies on many of their coins. In recent years several Arab rulers have also breached the regul-

ation and their portraits may be found on coins of Iraq (since 1931), Libya (1952), Kuwait (1976), Morocco (since 1956), Tunisia (since 1965), the United Arab Emirates (since 1964) and Jordan (since 1968). The Muslim ban on portraits of living creatures should not have been extended to cover historic personalities, but, none the less, very few have been depicted; Jinnah (Pakistan) and Soekarno (Indonesia) are among the notable exceptions. Turkey portrayed both Kemal Ataturk and Ismet Inonu in their lifetime and has continued to portray them, to the exclusion of other celebrities, ever since.

Top: Allegorical figures on republican coinage from French Oceania, Polynesia, Panama, Austria and Greece.

Above: Portraits on Islamic coins, in defiance of the edicts of the Prophet Mohammed: United Arab Emirates, Libya and Egypt.

Coins with Two Portraits

Coins bearing two portraits face to face are said to be *vis-à-vis* (using a French expression), or *bajoire* (from the French word baiser, to kiss). Some Roman coins have this feature but it was never popular as it wasted valuable space and was difficult to achieve satisfactorily. Nero issued an aureus in AD 54 with confronted busts of himself and his mother, Agrippina, portrayed as if they were the same age. It was only in the fifteenth century, when the greater availability of silver permitted larger and larger coins, that *vis-à-vis* portraits came into their own. Ferdinand of Aragon and Isabella of Castile set the trend with the excelente of 1497, which symbolized the union of two monarchs who ruled in their own right.

An excellent example is provided by the Austrian thalers of 1518, which bore confronted busts of the Emperor Maximilian I (1493–1519) and his grandson and successor Charles V (1519–58). From then onwards *vis-à-vis* portraits even extended to quite small coins. This was the style favoured by the English coins of 1554–8, which showed Queen Mary and her consort, King Philip II of Spain. The idea went out of favour again in the seventeenth century, one of the last issues being the coins of Château-Ren-

ault, which portrayed Louise-Marguerite of Lorraine and her husband, Francis of Bourbon, face to face. The coins were actually issued in 1625, but backdated to 1614, the year in which Francis died.

Full-face portraits side-by-side have seldom been used, mainly because it is very difficult to produce even one realistic portrait on a coin using a facing bust. In classical times, however, it was a popular device, especially in the Byzantine Empire, which produced many examples of this genre. The Byzantines established a curious fashion for coins, which portrayed the emperor and empress on the obverse, with two or more of their ancestors on the reverse, all full-face and side-by-side.

By far the most usual practice of portraying two or more persons is to show them side-by-side, one slightly overlapping the other. Such portraits are said to be jugate (from a Latin word meaning 'yoked together') or conjoined. Jugate profiles may be found on classical coins, from the staters of the Brutii (282–203 BC) to the bronze coins of Aretas IV of Nabataea in Arabia (9 BC–AD 40), as well as on the extensive issues of the Roman emperors. Jugate profiles made a comeback in the sixteenth century, as portraiture in general became more realistic. It became particularly

Below: England: silver half-crown of William III and Mary, (1693) showing conjoined busts on the obverse. The reverse has the four heraldic crowned shields of Great Britain, France and Ireland with the Lion of Orange in the centre. The date digits are in the angles between the shields which also bear the interlocking initials W and M.

Above right: Conjoined or jugate profiles on coins of Thailand and the UK, the latter portraying the Prince and Princess of Wales.

Below right: Heraldic coins from Tonga, Russia, Singapore, the Netherlands, Senegal and New Zealand.

fashionable in the German principalities where brothers often ruled jointly. The most celebrated coin of this type was the *Achtbruder* (eight brothers) thaler of Saxe-Weimer, 1605–19, which portrayed the eight sons of Duke Johan Ernst. Most of these coins have four brothers on each side but one rare version has eight of them on the same side. In Britain the use of conjoined profiles was confined to the period from 1689 to 1694 when William of Orange and Mary (daughter of James II) ruled jointly. After Mary's death William III was portrayed on his own. The crown issued by Britain in 1981 to celebrate the royal wedding, however, shows conjoined portraits of Prince Charles and Princess Diana on the reverse.

REVERSE MOTIFS

The Greek custom of featuring an attribute of a deity on the reverse had its counterpart in the allegorical designs on Roman coins. Because the Romans regarded coins as an important propaganda medium, the reverse designs were frequently changed. Not only did they symbolize Justice, Concord, Victory, Abundance and other abstract ideas, they frequently also depicted buildings and other public works and thus provided a unique record of Roman architecture. In the Dark Ages, coin reverses degenerated. In the Byzantine Empire, a cross, symbol of Christianity, was a very popular device and this was copied in Western Europe in medieval times. Not only did this serve as a Christian emblem, it provided a convenient guide when cutting coins into halves and quarters for use as small change. The cross was the dominant feature of English silver coins until the seventeenth century, although latterly it was often superimposed on a heraldic shield. A similar pattern existed elsewhere in Europe; the obverse was kept for the ruler's portrait but the reverse traditionally showed a Christian symbol, and latterly an emblem of the state.

National symbols continue to provide the main fare for coin reverses. Thus the current British decimal coins show a crowned portcullis on the 1p (first used on Tudor coins), the triple plumes of the Prince of

Right: UK: a proof set of the 1972 decimal coinage, including the Royal Silver Wedding crown and the Royal Mint's bronze plaquette.

Right: England: copper farthing of King Charles II. The figure of Britannia, based on a Roman coin of Antoninus Pius (138–61), was modelled by the Duchess of Richmond, one of the King's mistresses.

Wales on the 2p (used on many coins of the seventeenth century), a crowned thistle on the 5p (an emblem found on many old Scottish coins), a crowned lion passant guardant on the 10p (from the national coat of arms), a crowned rose on the 20p (first used on the crown of the rose issued by Henry VIII in 1526) and the seated figure of Britannia on the 50p (first used on the copper halfpennies and farthings of Charles II in 1672). Incidentally, the model for Britannia on these coins was the king's mistress, the Duchess of Richmond, but the design was actually based on a bronze sestertius of the Roman emperor Antoninus Pius (AD 138–61) to celebrate the advance of the Empire as far as the Forth-Clyde isthmus in Scotland.

When the pound coins were introduced in 1983, it was decided to place the English royal arms on the reverse, but in each succeeding year a different heraldic motif has been used. Thus the 1984 design showed the Scottish thistle, while the 1985 pound bore a Welsh leek and the 1986 pound a flax plant symbolizing Northern Ireland. In 1987 an English oak tree was chosen, while a crowned shield was subsequently adopted in 1988. Incidentally, these motifs were matched by appropriate edge inscriptions, the Welsh pound being the first to bear a slogan in the Welsh language: PLEIDIOL WYF I'M GWLAD.

US coins followed the British pattern, with various figures of Liberty or the American eagle. European countries pursued a heraldic policy; indeed, the prevalence of coin names such as *écu* (France), *escudo* (Portugal) and *scudo* (Italy) reflects the use of an escutcheon (from the Latin *scutum*, a shield). Under the German Empire, the coins of each kingdom, duchy and principality portrayed the ruler on the obverse, but a standard reverse showed the imperial eagle. The smaller denominations, current throughout the empire, had the eagle on the obverse and the value on the reverse.

PICTORIALISM

Although symbols and heraldry continue to dominate coin design to this day, there has been a resurgence of pictorialism in fairly recent years. Not since classical times have coins presented such a picture gallery in miniature. Until this century, pictorialism was confined to large commemorative coins, while the everyday, circulating coins were usually prosaic in design. The US broke new ground in 1913 when James Earl Fraser designed a nickel with the head of an Indian

Below: USA: Pictorial reverses showing the Lincoln Memorial (1c), the American Eagle landing on the Moon ($1) and Monticello (5c).

chief on the obverse and a buffalo on the reverse. The Jefferson nickel, which superseded it in 1938, showed Jefferson's mansion, Monticello, on the reverse, and in 1959 the Lincoln cent came into line by featuring the Lincoln memorial in Washington on its reverse. The Franklin half dollar featured the Liberty bell, while the Eisenhower dollar showed an eagle (emblem of the Apollo XI mission) landing on the moon.

In 1928, the Irish Free State replaced British coins with its own distinctive series. The harp of Ireland appeared on the obverse, but each reverse featured animals and birds: woodcock (farthing), sow and piglets (halfpenny), hen and chickens (penny), hare (threepence), wolfhound (sixpence), bull (shilling), salmon (florin) and horse (half crown). The 'Barnyard' series, as it was popularly known to collectors, broke new ground in realism and simplicity. The fashion for pictorial motifs spread to the UK with the series intended for King Edward VIII in 1936, but never

issued because of his abdication. The motifs were retained for the coins of his successor, George VI, in 1937 and included a wren (farthing), Sir Francis Drake's ship *Golden Hind* (halfpenny) and a thrift plant (nickel-brass threepence).

In 1938–9, Australia adopted a similar policy, introducing the kangaroo (halfpenny and penny), ears of wheat (threepence) and merino ram (shilling). Canada began using pictorial reverses in 1935 when a dollar showing *voyageurs* in a canoe was introduced. This was followed in 1937 by lower denominations showing maple leaves (1c), a beaver (5c), the famous schooner *Bluenose* (10c) and a caribou (25c).

Nowadays many countries use the reverse of their coins to depict scenery and landmarks, fauna and flora, or aspects of industry and commerce. More than ever before, coins have become a vital medium for projecting a country's image as well as furnishing attractive souvenirs for tourists and visitors.

Below: Ireland: the so-called 'Barnyard' series, 1928. The Irish Free State appointed a committee chaired by the poet, W.B. Yeats, to select designs from the world's leading medallists. The English sculptor Percy Metcalfe won the contest with his seies depicting birds, animals and fish associated with Ireland's agricultural economy. The designs were retained in 1971 when Ireland introduced decimal currency.

Right: Pictorial reverse motifs: UK farthing (wren), halfpenny *(Golden Hind)* and threepence (thrift); Canada 1c (maple leaf), 5c (beaver), 10c (schooner *Bluenose)* and 25c (caribou); Australia penny (kangaroo) and shilling (merino ram).

LEGENDS AND INSCRIPTIONS

Collectors reserve the term 'legend' for any lettering that runs round the perimeter of a coin, and refer to lettering that runs across the surface in a straight line as an 'inscription'. Conversely, any lettering inscribed on the edge of the coin is known as an edge inscription. This may seem a rather subtle distinction, but it is particularly useful in giving verbal descriptions of coins.

Lettering in the Hellenic World

The earliest Greek coins bore no lettering and are said to be anepigraphic; their identity can only be deduced by the devices stamped on them. Athenian coins were instantly recognizable by the head of Athena and her owl, while Pegasus indicated Corinth, a turtle Aegina and a boy on a dolphin Tarentum. A notable exception to this, however, was the electrum stater of Miletus in Ionia, which featured a stag and was inscribed in Greek 'I am the badge of Phanes', this otherwise unrecorded individual having been the magistrate during whose period of office the coin was struck. Otherwise, only the occasional cryptic letter was used, eg a capital *theta* on coins of Phocaea and the ancient Q-shaped letter *koppa* on coins of Corinth. By the sixth century BC, however, Athenian coins were being inscribed ATHE, and in the fifth century other city-states were following suit.

The earliest inscriptions were rather haphazardly placed on the reverse, often consisting of groups of two or three letters at the top and bottom. By the fourth century, however, legends were appearing around the perimeter and this pattern has been standard ever since. Many of the coins from the Hellenistic kingdoms had very long and elaborate inscriptions, reciting the name and titles of the ruler, and to accommodate them the lettering appeared in straight lines, arranged like a square with the reverse motif in the middle. The Seleucids and Bactrians even had to resort to double-banking their inscriptions, one square within the other.

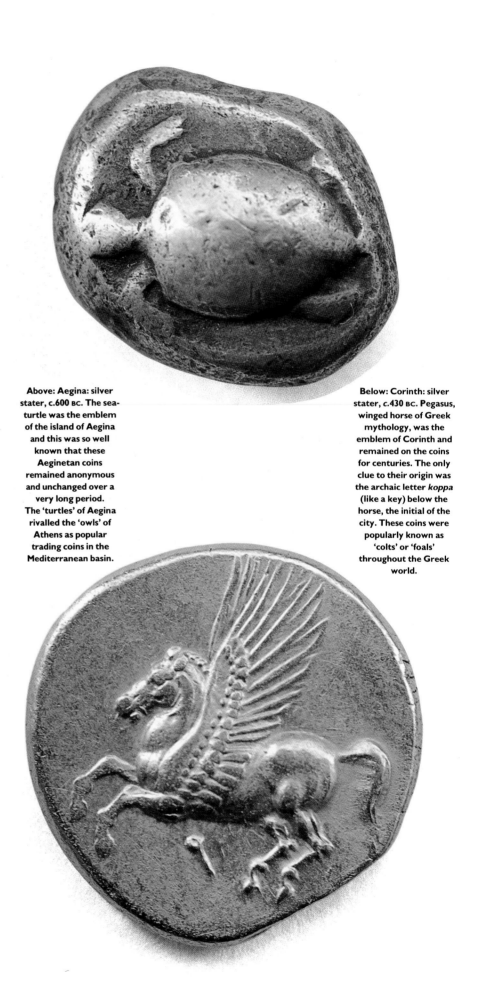

Above: Aegina: silver stater, c.600 BC. The sea-turtle was the emblem of the island of Aegina and this was so well known that these Aeginetan coins remained anonymous and unchanged over a very long period. The 'turtles' of Aegina rivalled the 'owls' of Athens as popular trading coins in the Mediterranean basin.

Below: Corinth: silver stater, c.430 BC. Pegasus, winged horse of Greek mythology, was the emblem of Corinth and remained on the coins for centuries. The only clue to their origin was the archaic letter *koppa* (like a key) below the horse, the initial of the city. These coins were popularly known as 'colts' or 'foals' throughout the Greek world.

Above: Tarentum: silver stater, fifth century BC. The legendary founder of the city was Taras, the original boy on a dolphin, and this was the motif which graced the city's coins.

Below: Great Britain: reverse of a shilling of King George II showing the abbreviations of his many titles.

Roman Inscriptions

It never seems to have occurred to the Greeks and their successors to spread the inscription to the obverse as well; that was left to the Romans. By the first century BC, rudimentary legends were appearing on the obverse, but reverse inscriptions were often confined to the exergue. This is the segment at the foot of the reverse, divided from the rest of the field by a straight line. The British gold sovereign has the date in the exergue, while the current 50p coin has the numerals of value in this position.

In the last years of the Roman Republic, legends on both sides became longer and more complex, culminating in the coins of Octavian, which bore the legend DIVI IVLI F. (son of the divine Julius). Octavian defeated Antony at Actium in 31 BC and became master of the Roman world. He changed his name to Augustus and adopted the title of caesar from his great-uncle. This surname was subsequently used as an indication of imperial rank, and, in the forms czar and kaiser, survived into the present century. The titles on Roman coins included such abbreviations as TRP (*tribunicia potestas*, tribunician power), PM (*pontifex maximus*, chief priest), IMP (*imperator*, commander-in-chief) and – most important of all – COS (*consul*). This information was followed by Roman numerals which enable us to date coins to a particular year of the emperor's reign.

Initials and Cryptic Inscriptions

Many of the inscriptions on Roman coins are cryptic, being confined to a series of abbreviations and initials, so it takes a lot of practice and experience to be able to decipher their meaning. This custom was by no means confined to Roman coins; the coins of many German states in the seventeenth and eighteenth centuries present a bewildering array of letters. This system spread to Britain under George I and his successors. On the obverse the king's name was followed by D.G. M. BR. FR. ET HIB. REX F.D. This stood for the Latin legend *Dei Gratia Magnae Britanniae, Franciae et Hiberniae Rex, Fidei Defensor*, 'By the Grace of God, King of Great Britain, France and

Ireland, Defender of the Faith'. The claim to the French throne was first raised by King Edward III in the fourteenth century and led to the Hundred Years War. Although England lost its last French territory (Calais) in the reign of Mary Tudor, the French title continued to appear on British coins until 1800.

Henry VIII was given the title of Defender of the Faith by Pope Leo X in 1521 for upholding the papacy against Martin Luther. Although Henry himself broke with Rome in 1534, he kept the title. However, neither he nor his successors expressed it on their coins until the accession of the Hanoverian dynasty in 1714. George I already had a splendid array of titles, but he believed in putting them all on his coins. The reverse carried the overflow, expressed as a set of initials: BR. ET L. D. S.R.I. A. T. ET E., *Brunsviciensis et Luneburgensis Dux, Sacri Romani Imperii Archi-Thesaurarius et Elector,* 'Duke of Brunswick and Luneberg, High Treasurer and Elector of the Holy Roman Empire'. This was actually a fairly modest array of titles; the elector of Bavaria, the archbishop of Cologne and the count of the Rhine-Palatinate had even longer strings of letters in the legends of their coins.

To this day British coins have the obverse legends in Latin, although they have changed over the years. Coins of Edward VII, George V and George VI were inscribed BRITT. OMN. REX FID. DEF. IND. IMP., meaning 'King of all the Britains (ie the UK and the British territories overseas), Defender of the Faith and Emperor of India'. Political changes after the Second World War led to the omission of IND. IMP. after 1948 when India and Pakistan gained

their independence, while BRITT. OMN. was dropped in 1954 when the process of decolonialization got underway.

The Place of Origin

In the Dark Ages, the barbarian tribes that overran the Roman Empire imitated the Romans and tried to inscribe their coins in Latin. The silver deniers and pennies of the early medieval period generally bore on their reverse the name of the town where the coin was struck and even the name of the individual moneyer (a tradition dating back to ancient Greece and Rome). In Anglo-Saxon, Norman and Plantagenet England alone, over a hundred towns had their own mint, identified by the legend on the reverse, while the number of mints all over Europe must have run into thousands. Although the coining irons (dies) might be supplied from a central authority, the inscriptions and legends on the reverse were usually distinctive. The last moneyer to have his name on English coins was Robert de Hadelie, Abbot of Bury St Edmunds (*c* 1283), but as late as Tudor times several mint-masters were identified by their initials or personal marks. Oddly enough, the custom of moneyers' initials survived much longer in Europe, and was last used in the USSR as recently as 1927.

MARKS AND SYMBOLS

As governments everywhere became more centralized at the end of the Middle Ages, the number of mints fell rapidly. Even where two or more mints continued to operate, their coins were no longer identified by the name of the mint in full and the place of mint and moneyers' names in the reverse legend was occupied either by royal titles or some kind of motto (invariably in Latin and usually quoting from the Bible). The last English coins to bear a town name were the pennies of Philip II of Spain and Mary Tudor (1554–8). Thereafter, the place of striking was denoted solely by an initial letter or a symbol. These are known as mint-marks and they continue to appear on many coins to this day.

Above and below: UK: obverse and reverse of the bronze penny of King George V, 1919. The tiny letter H to the left of the date in the exergue identifies the Heaton Mint, Birmingham, which struck some of the pennies of 1912, 1918 and 1919. Pennies of 1918–19 with the letters KN denote the King's Norton Mint, Birmingham. Unmarked pennies, of course, were struck at the Royal Mint in London.

Mint-marks

The practice of marking coins varies widely from country to country. Modern British coins, for example, do not have a mint-mark if they are struck by the Royal Mint, formerly at Tower Hill in London but now at Llantrisant in South Wales, but certain bronze coins with a letter H beside the date were struck by Ralph Heaton of Birmingham, while others lettered KN were produced at King's Norton, Birmingham. To this day, the Birmingham Mint uses the letter H as a mint-mark on many of the coins that it strikes for overseas countries. Similarly, coins with the letters PM denote the Pobjoy Mint of Sutton, Surrey.

INTERNATIONAL MINT-MARKS

France and Germany adopted a system of denoting individual mints by means of letters of the alphabet. Thus a French coin lettered A would have been struck at Paris, whereas C denoted Castelsarrasin and W Lille. At the present time, all coins are struck at the French Mint near Paris. Germany, however, continues to use several mints, and their coins may be recognized by the letters A (Berlin), D (Munich), F (Stuttgart), G (Karlsruhe) and J (Hamburg). Until recently, coins struck at the US Mint in Philadelphia were unmarked, but the letter P now denotes certain issues. The branch mints, on the other hand, are, or were, denoted by initial letters such as C (Charlotte), CC (Carson City), D (Dahlonega or Denver), O (New Orleans, S (San Francisco) and W (West Point). This system of identifying branch mints by means of their initials was also used to distinguish gold sovereigns and half sovereigns struck at Sydney (S), Melbourne (M) and Perth (P) in Australia, and at Ottawa, Canada (C), Calcutta, India (I) and Pretoria, South Africa (SA).

Right: German coins showing the D, F, G and J mint-marks of Munich, Stuttgart, Karlsruhe and Hamburg, and a Swiss coin with the B mint-mark of Berne.

Difference or Sequence Marks

Unfortunately, the term 'mint-mark' is also used rather loosely by collectors to denote a letter or symbol that ought more properly to be known as a difference mark or a sequence mark. In England, for example, these marks began appearing on coins in the reign of Edward III and were associated with the Trial of the Pyx, which was held annually in the Chapel of the Pyx at Westminster Abbey, but which nowadays is held each year in Goldsmith's Hall. This was the ceremonial testing of the purity and weight of certain gold and silver coins set aside in special boxes (*pyxis*). The symbols that appeared on coins denoted a period between each trial, and as these trials were held at more or less annual intervals, they are invaluable in helping collectors to date coins from an era before dates were actually inscribed. These marks survived on English coins until the last of the hammered coinage in 1662, but as dates had been creeping in for over a century previously, they had gradually become redundant.

Below: France: 5 francs of 1843 showing *marques et différents* at the foot. The lamb and flag (left) and B (right) are, respectively, the privy marks of the mint director and the mint-mark of Rouen, while the dog's head below the knot is the privy-mark of the Engraver General.

These marks generally appeared on both obverse and reverse, at the beginning of the legend (about one o'clock). It is interesting to note that, in 1983, the Royal Mint revived a mark of this sort, in the form of a long cross *fitchée*, to indicate the beginning of the incuse inscription on the edge of pound coins.

Above: Isle of Man: 5p coin (Laxey Wheel) showing the Millennium privy-mark, 1979.

Privy Marks

French coins bear two symbols, known to collectors as privy marks, although the official term in France is *Marques et Différ-ents*. These represent the men responsible for the dies. One series denotes the engraver general (or, since 1880, the chief engraver), while the other denotes the director of each mint. The engravers' marks are common to all coins, as the dies were supplied from central authority. In the past century, these marks have consisted of fasces (1880–96), torch (1896–1930), wing (1931–58), owl (1958–74) and fish (since 1974). The directors' marks, of

---

THE MARK OF A DESIGNER

In many cases, the name or initials of the designer or die engraver may also be found somewhere on the obverse or reverse, or even on both sides. This tradition goes back to the fifth century BC when certain large coins of Syracuse bore the abbreviated names of their engravers, Kimon and Euainetos. Many French coins bear the engraver's name or signature in full, but in the circulating coins of the UK the only man to have this honour was Benedetto Pistrucci whose surname can be seen on the silver crowns of 1818–20. This appears along the truncation of the king's neck on the obverse and in the exergue on the reverse. Hitherto, engravers and designers were not identified, but since then many artists have been denoted. B.P. (Pistrucci) appears on the St George and Dragon reverse of the gold coins to the present day; Victorian coins were inscribed W.W. (William Wyon), L.C.W. (Leonard Charles Wyon), J.E.B. (Joseph Edgar Boehm) or T.B. (Thomas Brock); while Edwardian coins bore the initials DE S. (George De Saulles). During the present reign, eight different sets of designers' initials have been used, but at least six other designers have remained anonymous.

Above: Great Britain: half-crown of 1723 showing the provenance mark of the South Sea Company, the initials SSC in the angles between the heraldic shields.

Below: Great Britain: half-crown of 1712 showing the provenance marks of the Company for Smelting Pit Coale and Sea Coale, roses and plumes in alternate angles.

Below: Great Britain: crown of George II, 1746 with **LIMA** below the truncation of the King's bust. Above: close-up of the obverse showing **LIMA**.

Above: England: close-up of the guinea of James II showing the elephant and castle emblem of the Africa Company at the foot of the obverse.

Below: England: guinea of James II (first bust, 1685) showing the elephant and castle emblem below the truncation of the King's neck.

course, vary from mint to mint but as the number of mints dwindled, so also did the range of directors' marks. Marseilles and Lille closed down in 1857 and Bordeaux in 1878, leaving only Paris. The bee (symbol of the Bonaparte family) appeared on Parisian coins from 1861 to 1879, but during the Commune of 1871 the mint was under the control of Citizen Camélinat, whose privy mark was a trident. Only 5 franc coins were minted during this revolution and most were melted down after Paris was liberated by the Thiers regime. From 1880 the symbol represented the office rather than the director, and therefore only a cornucopia has been used ever since.

The term privy mark is also used at the present time for symbols added to the design of a definitive coin of a permanent series in order to convert it into a commemorative piece. Good examples of this will be found on Manx coins bearing a circular triskelion (Millennium of Tynwald, 1979) or a baby's crib (birth of Prince William, 1982). In some cases, privy marks have appeared as sets of initials, for example the pound coins of 1980 inscribed on the reverse D.M.I.H.E. to indicate distribution at the *Daily Mail* Ideal Homes Exhibition of that year.

Below: Great Britain: obverse of the Queen Anne crown of 1703. Above: Close-up of the obverse showing VIGO at the foot.

Provenance Marks

Provenance marks are letters or symbols that identify the source of the metal. The best-known examples of this in British coinage are the gold and silver of 1703, with the word VIGO below Queen Anne's bust, and the coins of George II dated 1745–6, inscribed LIMA. Such coins were struck from Spanish bullion seized by an Anglo-Dutch expedition to Vigo Bay in 1702, and by Admiral Anson during his round-the-world voyage of 1740–4.

Bullion from the Guinea coast, supplied by the Africa Company, was denoted by the company badge of an elephant or an elephant and castle (1663–1722). Silver coins of George I inscribed S.S.C. came from bullion of the ill-fated South Sea Company which went bust in 1720, while coins inscribed W.C.C. below the king's neck (obverse) and having interlinked CC in alternate quadrants (reverse) denoted silver from the Welsh Copper Company. Silver coins with English roses and Welsh plumes on the reverse indicated bullion supplied by the quaintly named Company for Smelting Pit Coale and Sea Coale. Gold coins of George II, produced from metal supplied by the East India Company, bore the initials E.I.C.

Above: UK: close-up of the reverse of the sovereign, showing the die numbers 23 between the knot of the wreath and the heraldic flowers.

Below: UK: reverse of the 'Shield-back' sovereign of Queen Victoria, showing die numbers at the foot.

Control Marks

Control marks are sometimes used to denote the particular ingots from which the coin blanks were cut. This system, using letters or numerals, goes back to 265 BC when Egyptian silver didrachms were thus marked. This practice was used at Athens (second and first centuries BC) and on the coins of the Roman Republic. It has its modern counterpart in the British gold and silver coins of 1863–80, which have tiny numerals on the reverse, identifying the particular die used. In recent years, many coins of the Isle of Man and Gibraltar have had security die marks, in the form of two capital letters in various combinations discreetly concealed in the design. Early in 1937, Canada issued 1c, 10c and 25c coins dated 1936 but with a dot below the wreath to distinguish this emergency issue from the normal production of the previous year. Of the 678,823 cents struck, only eight were actually issued, while of the 192,194 dimes struck, only four are now believed to be in existence.

Above: UK: obverse of the gold sovereign of 1865 with the Young Head portrait of Queen Victoria. The engraver's initials W.W. (William Wyon) can be seen on the truncation of the Queen's neck.

Below: Security die marks on the reverse of the Gibraltar 50p (bottom left) and Isle of Man five-pound coin, 1973 (runic letters inscribed on the rock below the horse's hooves).

DATES

Apart from the legend identifying the issu-ing authority, and the words or numerals signifying the value, the other invariable feature of modern coins is a date. Nowadays the date is usually rendered as four digits in the modified Arabic numerals used in European scripts. Less frequently encoun-tered are examples using Roman numerals, although there was a brief vogue for this in mid-nineteenth-century Britain. The Una and the Lion pattern five pounds of 1839 had the date rendered as MDCCCXXIX in the exergue, and this date was retained in 1989 for a series of gold coins issued by Gibraltar, modelled on William Wyon's cele-brated design. The florins from 1849 to 1887 had their dates in Roman numerals rendered in Gothic script. This was the style used for the first English dated coin, the shilling issued by Edward VI in 1548. Three years later, the first silver crown bore the date in Arabic numerals – 1551 – above the shield on the reverse. A few European coins of the fifteenth century bore a date of this kind, but dates did not become common in Europe until the seventeenth century.

Earlier coins could be dated approx-imately from the sequence marks denoting Trials of the Pyx. Alternatively, a reference might be made to a regnal year, with the Latin formula ANNO REGNI (in the year of

Below: UK: gold sovereign of 1910 and bronze penny of 1967, showing dates in the exergue.

DATING FROM MUHAMMAD'S FLIGHT

The coins of the Islamic countries compensated for their lack of por-traiture or pictorialism by having lengthy legends and inscriptions that included the date. The date was usually preceded by an Arabic formula such as 'In the year of the Hijra of the Prophet'. Not only the year, but often the month and even the day of issue were given, with dates rendered in words rather than numerals. Such precision was virtually unheard of in European coins. Islamic coins were dated in words until the fifteenth cen-tury but thereafter numerals came into use, as in Europe. Muslim dates are expressed in years from the Hijra, or flight of Muhammad from Mecca. Moroccan coins had Muslim dates expressed in European numerals.

the reign) followed by Roman numerals. Regnal years of this kind may be found on the edge of crowns of George III, although the date in numbers is shown on the reverse. Coins dated 1818 and 1819 can be found with *two* regnal dates, as the regnal year did not coincide with the calendar year.

Below: UK: obverse of the Victorian copper penny of 1858, and a close-up showing the date at the foot and (above) the engraver's initials **W.W.** on the truncation of the Queen's neck.

The practice of dating coins also differs widely from country to country. At one extreme is the US where federal law requires coins to bear the year in which they are actually struck, while in many other countries coins continue to bear the date of the year in which they were first struck. Sometimes a compromise is effected, hence the 'dot' coins of Canada already mentioned. The same thing happened in 1948 when coins dated 1947 were struck with a tiny maple leaf emblem alongside the date. This was because the 1948 dies, omitting IND IMP from the legend, were at that stage not available.

From 1868 to 1982 most Spanish coins bore two dates. The larger date was the year of authorization, while the actual year of minting was denoted by way of a six-pointed star on which a minuscule date was inscribed incuse.

Occasionally the last digit on a coinage die is altered to a later date merely by striking over it with a numeral punch. Coins minted from emended dies of this sort are termed overstrikes or overdates and many instances have been recorded in both British and American coinage of the nineteenth century.

Kinds of Coins

ost of the coins mentioned so far are the kind that were intended for everyday use – the definitive, permanent issues designed for general circulation. In bygone times there were various by-products of coin preparation and these have always been much sought after by collectors.

PROOFS

Sometimes a design will actually get as far as the engraving of dies, but the issue may not proceed. Any pieces struck from these dies are regarded as essays, trial pieces or patterns. In some cases, the differences between patterns and the issued coins are very slight, but in many other instances the patterns are quite unlike anything subsequently issued. This often occurs when a mint, in quest of a coinage contract, goes as far as to produce samples of what the coins could look like, but then a rival mint obtains the work. Sometimes patterns are prepared for a parliamentary or congressional committee investigating proposed changes in coinage. Some patterns may be selected and will progress to the stage of actual issue, but others will be rejected. As a rule, patterns are rare because no more than a handful may have been struck.

Trial strikes, to test the dies and ensure that every detail is correct, are known as proofs. Originally, proofs were no more than that, and they were often pulled on a type of metal other than that intended for the issued coins. Lead was a favourite medium because of its softness. Because

proofs were carefully struck one at a time rather than mass-produced in high-speed presses, they were often of better quality than the normal coins. Blanks were specially prepared with a mirror finish, and the dies were often frosted so that the relief would stand out matt in contrast. In the eighteenth and nineteenth centuries, proofs were often struck in small quantities for presentation to mint officials and government ministers, and out of this charming custom arose the notion of producing proof sets for sale to collectors. This has become a very lucrative business in recent years. Indeed, it has reached the point in some countries where coins are only available in proof condition!

Proof coins can usually be distinguished by their superior finish, but nowadays they are often struck in precious metals, whereas their counterparts, destined for ordinary circulation, will be minted in base metals. Coins minted in metals other than those

Above: Scotland: pattern crown of James VIII (the Old Pretender) at the time of the Jacobite Rebellion of 1715.

Below: Isle of Man: the pound coin as issued in virenium (right), together with a pattern (left) in a different alloy and showing the compass point N which was omitted in the issued version.

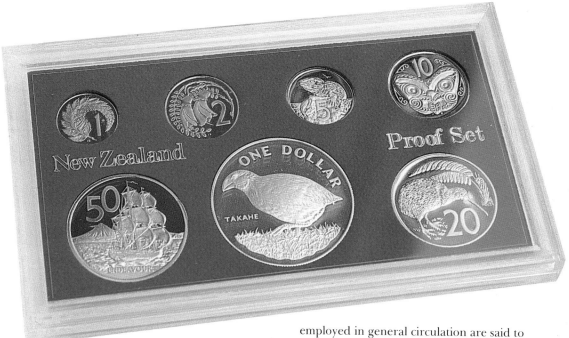

Above: New Zealand: the proof set of 1982, including the silver version of the Takahe dollar.

employed in general circulation are said to be off-metal strikes (OMS for short). There is also an intermediate version, which has developed in recent years. This is struck in the same base metal alloy as the ordinary coins but in a superior finish. Mints have invented various terms to describe this, such as 'specimen', 'library' or 'diamond' finish. These coins are usually packaged in some way to protect them, but perhaps not always inserted in plush-lined leather cases, as has traditionally been the practice for proof coins. A good number of countries now issue year sets, either in specimen finish or as proofs, or both, and these offer a straightforward method of acquiring new coins in mint condition.

Right: Australia: presentation folder containing the 1989 year set.

COMMEMORATIVE COINS

Apart from the coins intended for general circulation over a period of years, there are other special issues of various sorts. Commemorative coins date back to 510 BC when Elis began striking coins for the four-yearly Olympic Games. Many of the so-called 'large brass' of the Roman Empire celebrated a victory, the inauguration of some public building or an event of great importance. In the Middle Ages, when coins were quite utilitarian in design and execution, there was little inclination to use them to celebrate a particular event, although English silver pennies of the late tenth century, which parted company from standard practice by depicting the Lamb of God, may have been intended to celebrate the millennium of Christianity.

Left: Canada: Winter Olympics $20, 1985, silver proof with frosted relief on a mirror table.

Below: Canada: silver proof dollar in a red plush presentation case. The reverse of this coin reproduces the painting *The Fathers of Confederation*.

WHY 'DOLLAR'?

In 1519, the Counts of Schlick began striking large silver guldengroschen. They could afford to do so because their silver mines at Joachimsthal in Bohemia (now Jachymov in Czechoslovakia) were among the richest in Europe. These beautiful large coins were nicknamed Joachimsthalers, but this was soon shortened to 'thaler'. The term was applied to any large silver coin and it spread to other countries, which modified the word to suit their own languages. Thus it became a talar in Saxony, a tallero in Italy, a talari in Ethiopia and a tala in Samoa. In Denmark, however, it became a daler and in Holland a daalder, while in English it eventually emerged as a dollar. This name was applied to the Spanish peso de a ocho reales – the 'pieces of eight' associated with the pirates and buccaneers of the Spanish Main.

The Holy Roman Empire

While the Spanish dollars tended to stick to the same motifs, with the heraldic interpretation of the Pillars of Hercules (Straits of Gibraltar) and the Latin motto PLUS ULTRA (more beyond, meaning America), the thalers issued by the numerous kingdoms, principalities, duchies, free cities, margravates and bishoprics of the Holy Roman Empire and its neighbours vied with each other in their imaginative motifs. Many of these beautiful coins are classed as *Ausbeutethaler*, meaning that their design refers to the source of the metal used, either the particular mine or the river from which alluvial silver was dredged. A large and varied class of thalers commemorates royal events. Mourning thalers had a portrait of the dear departed on one side and the successor to the throne on the other. Then there were coins commemorating royal birthdays, weddings, coronations and jubilees. *Wahlmünzen* were coins that celebrated the election of a new holy Roman Emperor. *Schutzfestmünzen* or *Schiessthaler* were coins struck in Germany and Switzerland and given as prizes in annual shooting contests.

Bavaria was a very prolific issuer of commemorative thalers and, between 1825 and 1849, produced no fewer than 41 different coins celebrating events as disparate as the Customs union with Württemberg (1827) and the parting of Prince Otto and his mother near Aibling on his election as King of Greece (1835).

The United States

The US began issuing commemorative coins in 1892, when a half dollar celebrated the quatercentenary of the discovery of America by Columbus. This was reissued in 1893 with a quarter-dollar honouring Queen Isabella of Spain. Considering the popularity of silver dollars in general, it seems strange that until very recently only one commemorative silver dollar was issued, to commemorate the Marquis de Lafayette (1900). It was not until 1983 that silver dollars were again used for commemorative purposes (the Los Angeles Olympic Games).

The preferred medium for commemorative coins in the US was the silver half dollar, of which 46 different types were minted up to 1954. Interest waned because it was felt that these coins had been overdone, and no further commemoratives were issued until 1976 when a modest set of three (quarter, half and dollar) were released to celebrate the bicentenary of Independence. These had the normal obverse design with double dates (1776–1976), but entirely new reverses were designed for the quarter and half dollar. Since 1982 there has been a resumption of commemorative half dollars, as well as a number of higher denominations, reflecting a relaxation in federal law, which now permits US citizens to possess gold coins.

The United Kingdom

The UK has pursued a very conservative policy with regard to commemoratives. The silver crown of five shillings was the ideal medium for this, beginning with the Silver Jubilee of 1935. Subsequent crowns celebrated the Festival of Britain (1951), the Coronation (1953) and Sir Winston Churchill (1965). Decimalized as 25 new pence, crowns were issued to commemorate the Silver Wedding (1972), the Silver Jubilee (1977), the 80th birthday of the Queen Mother (1980) and the wedding of the Prince and Princess of Wales (1981). When the crown was next issued, in 1990, it was revalued as a five pound coin and celebrated the Queen Mother's 90th birthday. Meanwhile, the UK has flirted with a commemorative 50p (to mark entry into the EEC in 1973) and two coins, for the Commonwealth Games (1986) and the tercentenaries of the Bill of Right and the Claim of Right (both 1988).

Above right: UK: reverse of the two-pound coin of 1986 celebrating the Commonwealth Games, Edinburgh, mounted in the official tartan folder.

Below right: UK: crowns celebrating the Festival of Britain (1951) and the Coronation of Queen Elizabeth II (1953).

Right and below: Coins supporting the 'Food for All' (FAO) campaign, from Thailand, the Isle of Man and Indonesia. The last-named also promoted family planning.

Below: Commemorative coins designed for general circulation: Canada (Mounties' centenary, 1973), New Zealand (centenary of settlement, 1940), Australia $1 (International Year of Peace) and Thailand 2 baht (Outstanding Leadership in Rural Development).

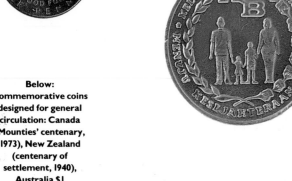

Base-metal Commemoratives

Not by any means are all commemoratives large, expensive coins in silver or gold. In recent years, many countries have issued base-metal circulating coins to publicize the 'Food for All' campaign of the UN Food and Agricultural Organization, although in many cases off-metal precious versions and proofs were also released. One could form a very interesting, yet quite inexpensive, collection devoted to base-metal commemoratives intended for general circulation. Canada has had several coins of this type, ranging from the nickel of 1951 (bicentenary of the nickel industry) to the quarter of 1973 (centenary of the Mounties). Thailand has been a prolific issuer of low-value commemoratives in recent years.

Below: Pobjoy Mint Christmas card encapsulating an Isle of Man Christmas 50p; the card reproduces in colour the scene depicted on the coin.

TOKENS

Most dictionaries define a token as a pledge or promise. In coinage, strictly speaking, a token is any coin whose intrinsic value is less than its notional or face value. Nowadays *all* coins are mere tokens, with little or no intrinsic value. Britain abandoned the tradition of coins of full intrinsic value at the time of the great coinage reform of 1816, took the process a step further in 1920 when silver was debased to 50 per cent and gold coins were withdrawn from circulation, and completed the process in 1946 when even debased silver was replaced by cupro-nickel. In practice, however, the term 'token' is reserved for subsidiary coinage that is not authorized by the government. Tokens are not legal tender in the sense of coins, but they serve the same purpose as coins with perhaps no more than local validity.

The Stuart monarchs made a half-hearted attempt to supply base-metal half-pence and farthings from 1672 onwards, but only after countless merchants and shopkeepers had taken the law into their own hands and issued lead, copper, brass, tin or pewter farthings. Over 4,000 tradesmen in London alone issued tokens, mostly in the period before the Great Fire of 1666, so they form an invaluable and unique record of the city that disappeared in that holocaust. A failure of the government to issue copper halfpence and farthings after 1775 led to the revival of tokens in 1787. They were suppressed in 1797 when the Cartwheel coinage was introduced, but in the space of a single decade an astonishing range of pennies, halfpence and farthings was produced. They were issued by most businesses, inns and taverns, shopkeepers and even local authorities and served both as small change and as advertisements for the issuers. Latterly they were even produced more or less for collectors, with thematic sets devoted to famous landmarks and historic personages. A shortage of silver coins during the Napoleonic wars led to a further spate of tokens which included sixpences and shillings as well as the base-metal pence and farthings. They were suppressed in 1816, at which time the coinage was completely overhauled.

Tokens were by no means confined to Britain. Many of the earliest coins of Australia, Canada, Ireland, the Isle of Man and Gibraltar resulted from the initiative of local merchants and bankers. In the US tokens were struck on two occasions. Between 1834 and 1844 the so-called 'Hard Time' tokens not only provided the public with small change but satirized the struggle between President Jackson and the United States Bank. There was a second period of tokens during the Civil War, when shopkeepers combined their own advertisements with patriotic motifs. During the First World War, tokens were issued in many countries, whether directly involved in the conflict or not. At the present time, tokens known as trade dollars are extremely popular in Canada where they are issued to celebrate all manner of events of local rather than national importance and are given a limited period of validity.

Many other kinds of tokens, while not actually valid as coins, have or once had a monetary value representing goods or services, or are encashable for coin of the realm. Into this category come transportation tokens, telephone tokens, gambling chips, co-operative tokens and checks and the tokens used by hotels, restaurants and public bars, gaming machines, laundromats, car-washes and many other service industries. Shopkeepers have given tokens to customers, redeemable in purchases at a later date. At least one trader, in Australia, even gives his customers interest-bearing tokens to keep pace with inflation. These are all eminently collectable and are of particular interest to the local collector. Over 300 types of pub token have been recorded for Wales alone.

Below: Canada: obverse and reverse of the brass token of the Hudson's Bay Company valued at one beaver pelt. The abbreviation NB at the foot was an error for MB (Made Beaver).

Below: Trade tokens of the eighteenth century: (right) Bath penny, (left) 'Ships, Colonies and Commerce' halfpenny intended for circulation in British North America.

Bibliography

American Numismatic Society, *America's Copper Coinage, 1783–1857*, New York, 1985

America's Silver Coinage, 1794–1891, New York, 1987

Angus, Ian, *Coins and Money Tokens*, Ward Lock/Fell, 1974

Becker, T.W., *The Coin Makers and the Development of Coinage from Earliest Times*, Doubleday, 1969

Bell, R.C., *Commercial Coins, 1787–1804*, Corbitt & Hunter, 1963

Berry, George, *Taverns and Tokens of Pepys' London*, Seaby, 1978

Bowers, Q. David, *Coins and Collectors*, Bowers & Merena Galleries, 1988

Bradley, H.W., *A Handbook of Coins of the British Isles*, Hale, 1984

Breen, Walter, *Complete Encyclopedia of US and Colonial Coins*, Doubleday, 1988

Broome, Michael, *A Handbook of Islamic Coins*, Seaby, 1985

Burnett, A., *Coinage in the Roman World*, Seaby, 1987

Carradice, I. and Price, M., *Coinage in the Greek World*, Seaby, 1988

Carson, R.A.G., *Coins, Ancient, Medieval and Modern*, Hutchinson, 1962

Clain-Stefanelli, Elvira, *Russian Gold Coins*, Spink, 1962

Coin World (ed.), *Coin World Almanac*, Amos Press, 1988

Cooper, D., *The Art and Craft of Coin-making*, Spink, 1988

Cresswell, O.D., *Chinese Cash*, Spink, 1971

Cribb, Joe (ed.), *Money, from Cowrie Shells to Credit Cards*, British Museum, 1986

Cribb, J., Cook, B. and Carradice, I., *The Coin Atlas*, Macdonald, 1990

Davis, Norman, *Greek Coins and Cities*, Spink, 1967

Doty, Richard G., *The Encyclopaedia Dictionary of Numismatics*, Macmillan, 1982

Dyer, Graham P., *The Royal Mint, an Illustrated History*, Royal Mint, 1986

Haxby, James, *Striking Impressions*, Royal Canadian Mint, 1984

Hoberman, Gerald, *The Art of Coins*, Spink/Lund Humphries, 1981

Hobson, Burton, *Coin Collecting as a Hobby*, Sterling, 1986

Jacob, Kenneth, *Coins and Christianity*, Seaby, 1984

Jenkins, *Ancient Greek Coins*, Seaby, 1990

Jones, John Melville, *A Dictionary of Ancient Roman Coins*, Seaby, 1990

Junge, Ewald, *World Coin Encyclopedia*, Barrie & Jenkins, 1984

Krause, Chester and Mishler, Clifford, *Standard Catalogue of World Coins*, Krause, 1988

Kroha, Tyll, *Lexikon der Numismatik*, Bertelsman, 1977

Linecar, Howard, *The Observer's Book of Coins*, Warne, 1977

British Coin Designs and Designers, Bell, 1977

McDonald, Greg, *Australian Coins and Banknotes*, McDonald, 1985

Mackay, James, *Greek and Roman Coins*, Arthur Barker, 1972

A History of Modern English Coinage, Henry VII to Elizabeth II, Longman, 1984

Key Definitions in Numismatics, Muller, 1982

Value in Coins and Medals, Johnson, 1968

Mays, James O'Donald, *The Splendid Shilling*, New Forest Leaves, 1982

Mira, William J.D., *From Cowrie to Kina*, Spink, 1986

O'Sweeney, James, *A Numismatic History of the Birmingham Mint*, Birmingham Mint, 1981

Plant, Richard, *Arabic Coins and how to Read Them*, Seaby, 1973

Greek Coin Types and their Identification, Seaby, 1979

Porteous, John, *Coins in History*, Weidenfeld & Nicholson, 1969

Pridmore, Major F., *The Coins of the British Commonwealth of Nations*, 4 vols, Spink, 1960–75

Purvey, Frank, *Collecting Coins*, Seaby, 1985

Reeds, Brian (ed.), *Coins of England and the United Kingdom*, Seaby, latest edition 1990

Reinfeld, Fred and Hobson, Burton, *A Catalogue of the World's Most Popular Coins*, Sterling, 1976

Reinfeld, Fred, *A Catalogue of European Coins*, Sterling, 1961

Room, Adrian, *A Dictionary of Coin Names*, Routledge, 1987

Schön, Günter, *World Coin Catalogue, Twentieth Century*, Seaby, 1985

Seaby, H.A. and Bussell, M., *British Copper Coins and Their Values*, Seaby, 1982

Seaby, H.A., *Greek Coins and Their Values*, Seaby, 1966

Seaby, Peter, *Coins and Tokens of Ireland*, Seaby, 1970

Coins of Scotland, Ireland and the Islands, Seaby, 1984

Sear, David, *Byzantine Coins and Their Values*, Seaby, 1974

Roman Coins and Their Values, Seaby, 1981

Greek Imperial Coins and Their Values, Seaby, 1982

Sutherland, H.C.V., *English Coinage, 600–1900*, Batsford, 1973

Swiatek, A. and Breen, H., *Silver and Gold Commemorative Coins*, Arco, 1981

Taxay, Don, *Counterfeit, Mis-struck and Unofficial US Coins*, Arco, 1963

An Illustrated History of US Commemorative Coinage, Arco, 1967

The US Mint and its Coinage, Arco, 1969

Travers, S.A., *Coin Collector's Survival Manual*, Arco, 1984

Whiting, J.R.S., *Trade Tokens – A Social and Economic History*, David & Charles, 1973

Whitting, P.D., *Byzantine Coins*, Barrie & Jenkins, 1963

Williamson, George, *Trade Tokens issued in the Seventeenth Century*, Spink, 1967

Yeoman, R.S., *The Handbook of United States Coins*, annual, Western Publishing

Index

Note. Captions to illustrations are indicated by *italic* page numbers.

PICTURE CREDITS

Grateful acknowledgement is made to B.A. Seaby Ltd. for providing coins for photography.

Thanks are also due to Adam Croton of Glendining's for the supply of supplementary illustrations on pages 9, 15 and 27.